Simple Guide to Programming with C++

Learn C++ Practical Guide

V.Telman

Copyright © 2024

Practical Guide

1.Introduction to C++

Overview of the C++ Language

C++ is a powerful and versatile programming language that has established itself as one of the most widely used and influential programming languages in the world. Created by Bjarne Stroustrup in the early 1980s as an extension of the C programming language, C++ introduced the concept of object-oriented programming (OOP), which allows programmers to create programs that are more modular, reusable, and easier to maintain. It retains all the efficiency and low-level control of C while adding features that allow for higher-level programming.

C++ is classified as a general-purpose, statically typed, and compiled language. This means it can be used to build a variety of applications across different domains, from systems programming, game development, and embedded systems to large-scale enterprise applications. The versatility of C++ comes from its blend of procedural, object-oriented, and generic programming paradigms.

C++ enables developers to write code that can directly

manipulate hardware resources, which is crucial for system-level programming, while also supporting high-level abstractions such as classes and templates. The language is highly portable and can be run on almost any platform, which is why it's often used for software that needs to run on multiple hardware architectures. One of the most notable features of C++ is its close association with the Standard Template Library (STL), which offers a rich set of generic classes and functions for handling data structures and algorithms.

Before delving deeper into the specifics of C++, let's take a look at how the language evolved and what differentiates it from other languages.

History of C++

The Origins in C

C++ is derived from the C programming language, which was developed by Dennis Ritchie at Bell Labs in the early 1970s. C itself was designed as a systems programming language, primarily intended for the development of the UNIX operating system. The main appeal of C was its simplicity, efficiency, and flexibility. It allowed low-level manipulation of memory and system resources while maintaining portability across different hardware platforms. However, C lacked certain features for structuring large, complex programs, especially those that required data abstraction and object-oriented design.

Bjarne Stroustrup and "C with Classes"

Bjarne Stroustrup, also working at Bell Labs, sought to build upon C's strengths while addressing its limitations, particularly in the area of structuring large software systems. In the late 1970s, Stroustrup began working on a language that would extend C with the features of Simula, an earlier programming language known for its pioneering use of object-oriented programming. Stroustrup initially referred to his language as "C with Classes" because he introduced the concept of classes and objects, which are central to object-oriented programming.

The first major version of C++ was released in 1983, and the name "C++" was adopted. The "++" symbol is a reference to the increment operator in C, signifying the language's evolution from C. Stroustrup's primary motivation was to create a language that was efficient like C but supported high-level abstractions for better program organization and design.

Key Milestones in the Evolution of C++

- **1985**: The first edition of Stroustrup's book *"The C++ Programming Language"* was published, marking the formal release of the language to the wider programming community.

- **1990**: The Annotated C++ Reference Manual was published, which became the foundation for the future standardization of C++.

- **1998**: C++ was standardized by the International Organization for Standardization (ISO) as ISO/IEC 14882:1998. This version is often referred to as C++98.

- **2003**: The standard was revised, leading to the C++03 version. The changes were mostly minor, fixing defects and clarifying ambiguities in C++98.

- **2011**: C++11 was released, bringing a major overhaul to the language. New features such as lambda expressions, the auto keyword, smart pointers, and concurrency support made C++11 a much more modern language, catering to both system-level and high-level programming needs.

- **2014**: C++14 refined many of the features introduced in C++11, providing additional improvements and bug fixes.

- **2017**: C++17 continued the trend of modernization by introducing features like structured bindings, if constexpr, and parallel algorithms in the STL.

- **2020**: C++20 is one of the most significant updates to the language since C++11, adding concepts, ranges, coroutines, and modules, making the language more expressive and safer to use.

Why C++ Remains Relevant

C++ has remained relevant for decades because it

successfully balances low-level system control with high-level programming abstractions. It allows developers to write highly efficient code, a key factor in industries like game development, finance, and high-performance computing, where speed and resource optimization are crucial. The language's constant evolution through new standards ensures that it remains modern, expressive, and capable of addressing the changing needs of software development.

C++ is also supported by a massive ecosystem of tools, libraries, and frameworks, making it a popular choice for both beginners and experienced programmers. Despite the emergence of new programming languages, C++ continues to be the foundation for many critical software systems.

Features of C++

C++ is a feature-rich language that brings together multiple programming paradigms and advanced features. Here are some of the most important features that make C++ stand out:

1. Object-Oriented Programming (OOP)

One of the key features that differentiate C++ from its predecessor, C, is its support for object-oriented programming. C++ introduces the concept of classes and objects, which allow developers to model real-world entities and relationships in their programs. OOP helps in better organizing code, improving reusability, and making the code more maintainable. The four pillars of OOP in C++ are:

- **Encapsulation**: Bundling data and methods that operate on the data within a single class.

- **Inheritance**: Creating new classes based on existing ones, enabling reuse and extension of code.

- **Polymorphism**: Allowing objects to be treated as instances of their parent class, enabling dynamic behavior at runtime.

- **Abstraction**: Hiding the internal complexity of objects and exposing only the necessary interface.

2. Low-Level Programming Capabilities

C++ maintains the close-to-the-hardware programming capabilities of C, which allows developers to write highly optimized code that can directly manipulate memory and hardware resources. This makes C++ ideal for systems programming, embedded systems, and performance-critical applications. Features like pointers, manual memory management, and inline assembly provide the necessary tools for low-level programming.

3. Generic Programming with Templates

C++ supports generic programming through its powerful template system. Templates allow developers to write code that can work with any data type. This is particularly useful for creating data structures and algorithms that are not tied to a specific type. The Standard Template Library (STL) is built on this feature and provides ready-made implementations of commonly used data structures (such as vectors, lists, and maps) and algorithms (such as sorting and searching).

4. Standard Template Library (STL)

The STL is a collection of generic classes and functions that provide implementations of many popular data structures and algorithms. It includes containers (like vector, list, and map), iterators (which provide a unified way to traverse through the elements of containers), and algorithms (such as sort, find, and search). STL is a key part of C++'s strength because it allows developers to use well-optimized, reusable components without having to reinvent the wheel.

5. Strongly Typed Language

C++ is a statically typed language, meaning that variable types are determined at compile time. This allows for early detection of type-related errors, leading to safer and more reliable code. C++ also supports strict type checking and conversions, ensuring that type-related errors are minimized.

6. Memory Management

One of the defining features of C++ is its support for manual memory management, which is critical for applications that need fine-grained control over resource usage. C++ uses operators like `new` and `delete` to allocate and free memory dynamically. This is in contrast to languages like Java or Python, which rely on automatic garbage collection. While manual memory management in C++ gives developers more control, it also introduces the potential for errors like memory leaks and dangling pointers, which require careful handling.

7. Multiple Paradigms

C++ is a multi-paradigm programming language. In addition to object-oriented programming, it also supports procedural programming (like C), functional programming (with features like lambdas and function pointers), and generic programming (with templates). This flexibility makes C++ suitable for a wide range of applications and programming styles.

8. Exception Handling

C++ provides robust support for error handling through exceptions. Exceptions allow developers to handle runtime errors in a structured way, preventing crashes and improving program reliability. The `try`, `throw`, and `catch` keywords form the basis of exception handling in C++. When an error occurs, an exception can be thrown, and the program can respond to it appropriately rather than terminating unexpectedly.

9. Operator Overloading

C++ allows operators like `+`, `-`, `*`, and `==` to be overloaded so that they can be used with user-defined types (such as classes). This feature enables more intuitive syntax when working with objects. For example, you can define how the `+` operator should behave when adding two complex numbers or concatenating two strings.

10. Namespace Support

Namespaces in C++ help to avoid naming conflicts, especially in large projects or when using third-party libraries. A namespace allows for the logical grouping of related code and ensures that names within different namespaces do not clash. For example, two functions named `foo()` can exist in two different namespaces, and the appropriate function can be invoked by specifying its namespace.

11. Concurrency Support

C++ has built-in support for multithreading and concurrent programming. With C++11 and later versions, the language introduced features like threads, mutexes, and atomic operations, making it easier to write programs that can take advantage of multi-core processors. These features are critical for building high-performance applications that need to execute tasks concurrently, such as in video games, real-time systems, or server applications.

Setting Up the Development Environment

Now that we've covered the theoretical aspects of C++, let's move on to the practical side. To start writing C++ programs, you need to set up a development environment. This includes installing a C++ compiler, configuring an Integrated Development Environment (IDE), and writing your first program.

Installing a C++ Compiler

A compiler is a program that translates your C++ source code into machine code that can be executed by your computer. There are several popular compilers available for C++, each with its own set of features and compatibility. Here are some of the most commonly used C++ compilers:

- **GCC (GNU Compiler Collection)**: This is a widely used open-source compiler that supports C, C++, and other languages. It's available on Linux, Windows (via MinGW or Cygwin), and macOS.

- **Clang**: A modern, open-source C++ compiler developed by the LLVM project. Clang provides fast compilation times and excellent error messages, making it a popular choice for many developers.

- **Microsoft Visual C++ Compiler**: Part of Microsoft's Visual Studio IDE, this compiler is widely used in the Windows ecosystem. It supports the latest C++ standards and is optimized for Windows development.

- **Intel C++ Compiler**: A high-performance compiler that is optimized for Intel processors. It is used in scientific and high-performance computing applications.

Installing GCC on Linux

For Linux users, GCC is often pre-installed, but if it's not, you can install it using the following commands:

```bash
sudo apt update
sudo apt install build-essential
```

This will install the GCC compiler along with other essential tools for building software.

Installing GCC on Windows (via MinGW)

To install GCC on Windows, you can use the MinGW (Minimalist GNU for Windows) toolchain. Follow these steps:

1. Go to the [MinGW website](http://www.mingw.org/) and download the MinGW

installer.

2. Run the installer and select the "gcc-g++" package.

3. Complete the installation and add the MinGW `bin` directory to your system's PATH variable, so you can use GCC from the command line.

Installing GCC on macOS

On macOS, you can install GCC via Homebrew, a popular package manager for macOS:

1. Install Homebrew if you haven't already:

   ```bash
   /bin/bash -c "$(curl -fsSL https://raw.githubusercontent.com/Homebrew/install/HEAD/install.sh)"
   ```

2. Install GCC:

   ```bash
   brew install gcc
   ```

Configuring an Integrated Development Environment (IDE)

An IDE combines a source code editor, compiler, debugger, and other tools into one package, making it easier to write, compile, and debug your programs. While it's possible to write and compile C++ code using a simple text editor and the command line, using an IDE can significantly improve productivity, especially for larger projects.

Here are some of the most popular C++ IDEs:

- **Visual Studio (Windows)**: Microsoft's Visual Studio is one of the most comprehensive and feature-rich IDEs for C++ development, especially for Windows-based applications. It comes with an integrated C++ compiler and supports debugging, refactoring, and code analysis.

- **CLion (Cross-platform)**: Developed by JetBrains, CLion is a cross-platform IDE that supports C and C++. It provides smart code completion, powerful refactoring tools, and an integrated debugger.

- **Code::Blocks (Cross-platform)**: A free, open-source C++ IDE that is lightweight and highly customizable. It supports multiple compilers, including GCC and Clang, and runs on Windows, macOS, and Linux.

- **Eclipse CDT (Cross-platform)**: Eclipse CDT (C/C++ Development Tooling) is an extension of the Eclipse IDE that adds support for C and C++ development. It's free and works on multiple platforms.

- **Xcode (macOS)**: Apple's Xcode IDE supports C++ development and is optimized for building macOS and iOS applications. It includes a powerful debugger and is integrated with Apple's developer tools.

Setting Up Visual Studio

To set up Visual Studio for C++ development:

1. Download and install [Visual Studio] (https://visualstudio.microsoft.com/).

2. During installation, select the "Desktop development with C++" workload.

3. Once installed, you can create a new C++ project from the "File" > "New" > "Project" menu.

Setting Up Code::Blocks

To set up Code::Blocks:

1. Download the [Code::Blocks IDE] (http://www.codeblocks.org/downloads).

2. Install it, and during installation, select the option to include a C++ compiler (if available).

3. Launch Code::Blocks and create a new C++ project.

Writing Your First C++ Program

Once you have your compiler and IDE set up, you can start writing your first C++ program. Let's go through a simple "Hello, World!" example, which is a standard introductory program in many programming languages.

1. Open your IDE and create a new C++ project.
2. Create a new C++ source file (`.cpp` file).
3. Write the following code:

```cpp
#include <iostream> // Include the iostream library for input/output operations

int main() {
    std::cout << "Hello, World!" << std::endl; // Output "Hello, World!" to the console
    return 0; // Return 0 to indicate that the program finished successfully
}
```

Explanation of the Code:

- `#include <iostream>`: This line includes the input/output stream library, which is necessary for using `std::cout` to print text to the console.

- `int main() { ... }`: The `main` function is the entry point of every C++ program. When the program is run, execution starts at `main`.

- `std::cout << "Hello, World!" << std::endl;`: This line uses the `std::cout` object to output the string "Hello, World!" to the console. The `std::endl` at the end inserts a newline character.

- `return 0;`: This indicates that the program has finished successfully. The return value `0` is sent to the operating system to signal that the program ended without errors.

Compiling and Running the Program

To compile and run the program:

1. Save your file with a `.cpp` extension.

2. Compile the program using your IDE's built-in compiler, or if you're using the command line, navigate to the directory containing the `.cpp` file and run:

```bash
g++ -o hello hello.cpp
```

This will create an executable file named `hello` (or `hello.exe` on Windows).

3. Run the executable:

```bash
./hello  # or hello.exe on Windows
```

You should see the output:

```
Hello, World!
```

Congratulations! You have successfully written, compiled, and executed your first C++ program.

C++ is a robust, versatile programming language that combines the efficiency and power of low-level programming with the abstractions of high-level programming paradigms. Its long history, ongoing evolution, and widespread usage across various domains make it an essential language for both beginners and experienced developers. Setting up a C++ development environment and writing your first program is the first step on a path toward mastering this language, which is used in everything from system programming and game development to scientific computing and real-time applications.

By understanding its history, features, and practical usage, you are well on your way to becoming proficient in C++.

2. Basics of C++ Programming

C++ is a powerful and versatile programming language that allows you to write efficient, maintainable, and scalable programs. Understanding the basics of C++ programming, such as its syntax, data types, operators, and control structures, is essential for developing high-quality software.

In this detailed guide, we will cover the fundamentals of C++ programming:

1. Syntax and Structure
2. Data Types and Variables
3. Operators and Expressions
4. Control Structures: Conditionals and Loops

1. Syntax and Structure

Basic Structure of a C++ Program

C++ programs follow a particular structure, which includes headers, the main function, statements, and, optionally, user-defined functions. Here's a basic template of a simple C++ program:

```cpp
Copia codice
#include <iostream>  // Header file for input-output operations
```

```
int main() {
    std::cout << "Hello, World!" << std::endl;  // Output statement
    return 0;  // Return 0 indicates successful program termination
}
```

Explanation of the Structure:

- **#include <iostream>**: This is a preprocessor directive that tells the compiler to include the standard input/output stream (iostream) library, which is needed for input and output operations like reading and writing to the console.

- **int main()**: Every C++ program must have a main() function. This is the entry point of the program where execution starts. The int before main indicates that this function returns an integer value.

- **std::cout << "Hello, World!"**: This is an output statement that prints the text "Hello, World!" to the console. std::cout is the standard output stream in C++. The << operator is used to send output to the console, and std::endl inserts a newline.

- **return 0;**: The main() function must return an integer value to the operating system when the program ends. Returning 0 typically indicates that the program executed successfully.

C++ Program Structure Breakdown

A typical C++ program consists of several components:

1. **Preprocessor Directives**: Preprocessor directives are instructions that are processed before the actual compilation starts. These are written at the top of the program and typically include header files, e.g., #include <iostream>. Preprocessor directives do not end with a semicolon.

2. **Main Function**: The main() function is where the execution of the program begins. Any C++ program must have exactly one main() function.

3. **Declarations and Statements**: Declarations define variables and other data types, while statements perform actions, such as computations, input/output operations, or function calls.

4. **Functions**: In addition to the main() function, a C++ program can have many user-defined functions to perform specific tasks.

Comments in C++

Comments are non-executable parts of the program that serve to explain the code. They are useful for documenting what the code does, making it easier to understand and maintain.

There are two types of comments in C++:

- **Single-line comments**: These start with // and extend to the end of the line.

    cpp
    Copia codice
    ```
    // This is a single-line comment
    ```

- **Multi-line comments**: These start with /* and end with */, spanning multiple lines if necessary.

    cpp
    Copia codice
    ```
    /* This is a multi-line comment.
       It can span across multiple lines. */
    ```

Whitespace and Indentation

C++ ignores extra whitespace (spaces, tabs, and newlines) between tokens, making it flexible in formatting. However, proper use of indentation is critical for readability and understanding the program's structure.

cpp
Copia codice
```
int main() {
    int x = 5;     // Indentation improves readability
    int y = 10;
    std::cout << x + y << std::endl;
```

```cpp
    return 0;
}
```

Blocks of Code

In C++, a block of code is defined by curly braces {}. It groups multiple statements together, which can be used in control structures, function definitions, or loop bodies.

cpp
Copia codice
```cpp
if (x > 0) {
    std::cout << "x is positive" << std::endl;  // Block of code
}
```

2. Data Types and Variables

Data Types in C++

Data types define the type of data that a variable can hold. C++ provides a rich set of built-in (or primitive) data types and allows you to define your own types using classes and structures.

Built-in Data Types

1. **Integer Types**: Used to represent whole numbers.

    - **int**: Typically 4 bytes in size, used for general-purpose integers.
    - **short**: Usually 2 bytes, for smaller

integers.
- **long**: 4 or 8 bytes, for larger integers.
- **long long**: At least 8 bytes, used for very large integers.

Example:

```cpp
Copia codice
int age = 25;
short year = 2021;
long population = 7000000000;
```

2. **Floating-point Types**: Used to represent numbers with fractional parts.
   - **float**: Typically 4 bytes, single-precision floating-point.
   - **double**: 8 bytes, double-precision floating-point.
   - **long double**: At least 8 bytes, for extended-precision floating-point.

Example:

```cpp
Copia codice
float pi = 3.14f;
double gravity = 9.81;
```

3. **Character Type**: Represents individual characters.
   - **char**: Typically 1 byte, stores a single

character or a small integer.

Example:

cpp
Copia codice
char letter = 'A';

4. **Boolean Type**: Represents truth values.

    - **bool**: Typically 1 byte, can hold either true or false.

Example:

cpp
Copia codice
bool isOpen = true;

5. **Void Type**: Represents the absence of a type. It is mainly used in function declarations where no value is returned.

Example:

cpp
Copia codice
void displayMessage() {
    std::cout << "This function does not return a value" << std::endl;
}

Derived Data Types

C++ also supports more complex types derived from the built-in types, including arrays, pointers, references, and enumerations.

- **Arrays**: An array is a collection of elements of the same type.

  Example:

  cpp
  Copia codice
  ```
  int numbers[5] = {1, 2, 3, 4, 5};
  ```

- **Pointers**: A pointer is a variable that stores the memory address of another variable.

  Example:

  cpp
  Copia codice
  ```
  int num = 10;
  int* ptr = &num;  // Pointer to the variable num
  ```

- **References**: A reference is an alias for another variable.

  Example:

  cpp
  Copia codice
  ```
  int a = 5;
  int& ref = a;  // ref is a reference to a
  ```

- **Enumerations**: An enumeration is a user-defined type that consists of a set of named integral constants.

Example:

cpp
Copia codice
enum Direction {North, East, South, West};
Direction dir = North;

Variables in C++

A variable is a named location in memory that stores a value. Before using a variable in C++, it must be declared with a specific data type.

Variable Declaration and Initialization

Variables are declared by specifying the data type followed by the variable name. Optionally, you can also assign an initial value.

cpp
Copia codice
int x;   // Declaration without initialization
x = 10;   // Assignment of value

int y = 20;   // Declaration with initialization

Rules for Naming Variables

- Variable names must begin with a letter
- (upper or lower case) or an underscore (_).
- After the first character, variable names can contain letters, digits, and underscores.
- Variable names are case-sensitive (age, Age, and AGE are distinct names).

- Reserved keywords (like int, return, for, etc.) cannot be used as variable names.

Constant Variables

C++ allows the declaration of constant variables whose values cannot be changed after initialization. This is done using the const keyword.

cpp
Copia codice
const int MAX_USERS = 100; // MAX_USERS cannot be modified

Type Conversion

C++ supports both implicit and explicit type conversion.

- **Implicit Conversion**: The compiler automatically converts one data type to another when necessary.

    Example:

    cpp
    Copia codice
    int a = 10;
    double b = a; // Implicit conversion from int to double

- **Explicit Conversion (Type Casting)**: You can explicitly convert one type to another using cast operators.

Example:

```cpp
Copia codice
double x = 5.67;
int y = (int)x;  // Explicit conversion from double to int
```

---

3. Operators and Expressions

Operators in C++ are symbols that perform operations on variables and values. They can be classified into several categories: arithmetic, relational, logical, bitwise, assignment, and others.

Arithmetic Operators

Arithmetic operators perform basic mathematical operations.

Operator	Description	Example
+	Addition	a + b
-	Subtraction	a - b
*	Multiplication	a * b
/	Division	a / b
%	Modulus	a % b (for integers)

Operator	Description	Example
	(remainder)	

Example:

```cpp
Copia codice
int a = 10;
int b = 3;
int sum = a + b;        // sum = 13
int difference = a - b; // difference = 7
int product = a * b;    // product = 30
int quotient = a / b;   // quotient = 3
int remainder = a % b;  // remainder = 1
```

Relational Operators

Relational operators compare two values and return a boolean result (true or false).

Operator	Description	Example
==	Equal to	a == b
!=	Not equal to	a != b
>	Greater than	a > b
<	Less than	a < b
>=	Greater than or equal	a >= b

Operator	Description	Example
	to	
<=	Less than or equal to	a <= b

Example:

cpp
Copia codice
int x = 5, y = 10;
bool result = (x < y); // result is true because 5 is less than 10

Logical Operators

Logical operators are used to combine or negate boolean expressions.

Operator	Description	Example
&&	Logical AND	a && b
`	`	`
!	Logical NOT	!a

Example:

cpp
Copia codice

```
bool a = true;
bool b = false;

bool result1 = a && b;  // result1 is false
bool result2 = a || b;  // result2 is true
bool result3 = !a;      // result3 is false
```

Assignment Operators

Assignment operators assign values to variables.

Operator	Description	Example
=	Assigns right operand to left operand	x = y
+=	Adds and assigns	x += y (equivalent to x = x + y)
-=	Subtracts and assigns	x -= y (equivalent to x = x - y)
*=	Multiplies and assigns	x *= y (equivalent to x = x * y)
/=	Divides and assigns	x /= y (equivalent to x = x / y)
%=	Modulus and assigns	x %= y (equivalent to x = x % y)

Example:

```cpp
Copia codice
int x = 5;
x += 10;  // x is now 15
x *= 2;   // x is now 30
```

Increment and Decrement Operators

Increment and decrement operators are used to increase or decrease a variable's value by 1.

Operator	Description	Example
++	Increment by 1	++x or x++
--	Decrement by 1	--x or x--

Example:

```cpp
Copia codice
int x = 5;
x++;  // x is now 6
--x;  // x is now 5
```

---

4. Control Structures: Conditionals and Loops

Control structures determine the flow of execution of a program based on certain conditions or repeat certain blocks of code multiple times.

Conditionals

Conditionals allow you to execute code based on certain conditions.

The if Statement

The if statement is used to execute a block of code only if a specified condition is true.

cpp
Copia codice
```
if (condition) {
    // Code to execute if condition is true
}
```

Example:

cpp
Copia codice
```
int x = 10;
if (x > 5) {
    std::cout << "x is greater than 5" << std::endl;
}
```

The if-else Statement

The if-else statement adds an alternative block of code that runs when the condition is false.

cpp
Copia codice
```
if (condition) {
    // Code to execute if condition is true
} else {
```

```
    // Code to execute if condition is false
}
```

Example:

```cpp
Copia codice
int x = 3;
if (x > 5) {
    std::cout << "x is greater than 5" << std::endl;
} else {
    std::cout << "x is not greater than 5" << std::endl;
}
```

The else-if Ladder

When multiple conditions need to be checked, you can use the else-if ladder.

```cpp
Copia codice
if (condition1) {
    // Code if condition1 is true
} else if (condition2) {
    // Code if condition2 is true
} else {
    // Code if none of the above conditions are true
}
```

Example:

```cpp
Copia codice
```

```cpp
int x = 7;
if (x > 10) {
   std::cout << "x is greater than 10" << std::endl;
} else if (x == 7) {
   std::cout << "x is 7" << std::endl;
} else {
   std::cout << "x is less than 10 and not equal to 7" << std::endl;
}
```

The switch Statement

The switch statement allows you to execute one block of code out of many based on the value of a variable.

cpp
Copia codice
```cpp
switch (expression) {
   case constant1:
      // Code to execute if expression equals constant1
      break;
   case constant2:
      // Code to execute if expression equals constant2
      break;
   default:
      // Code to execute if no case matches
}
```

Example:

cpp
Copia codice
```cpp
int day = 3;
```

```cpp
switch (day) {
   case 1:
      std::cout << "Monday" << std::endl;
      break;
   case 2:
      std::cout << "Tuesday" << std::endl;
      break;
   case 3:
      std::cout << "Wednesday" << std::endl;
      break;
   default:
      std::cout << "Invalid day" << std::endl;
}
```

Loops

Loops allow you to repeat a block of code multiple times.

The while Loop

The while loop repeats a block of code as long as the specified condition is true.

cpp
Copia codice
```cpp
while (condition) {
   // Code to execute as long as condition is true
}
```

Example:

cpp
Copia codice

```cpp
int i = 0;
while (i < 5) {
   std::cout << i << std::endl;
   i++;
}
```

The do-while Loop

The do-while loop is similar to the while loop, but it guarantees that the code inside the loop will run at least once, even if the condition is false.

cpp
Copia codice
```cpp
do {
   // Code to execute
} while (condition);
```

Example:

cpp
Copia codice
```cpp
int i = 0;
do {
   std::cout << i << std::endl;
   i++;
} while (i < 5);
```

The for Loop

The for loop is commonly used when the number of iterations is known beforehand.

cpp

Copia codice
```
for (initialization; condition; update) {
   // Code to execute
}
```

Example:

cpp
Copia codice
```
for (int i = 0; i < 5; i++) {
   std::cout << i << std::endl;
}
```

Understanding the basics of C++ programming, including its syntax, data types, operators, and control structures, forms the foundation for writing efficient and effective programs. By mastering these concepts, you can move on to more advanced topics such as object-oriented programming, memory management, and advanced data structures.

3. Functions in C++

Functions are fundamental building blocks in any programming language, including C++. They allow code reuse, improve program organization, and simplify complex problems by dividing them into smaller, manageable tasks. In C++, functions enable modular programming, making the code easier to read, maintain, and debug. This guide will explore the intricacies of functions in C++, including how to define and call them, function overloading, argument passing mechanisms (by value and by reference), and the concept of template functions.

1. Defining and Calling Functions

A function in C++ is a block of code that performs a specific task. Functions have a name, a return type, parameters (optional), and a body containing the statements that define the function's behavior.

Defining a Function

To define a function in C++, you specify:

1. **Return type**: The type of value the function will return. It could be any data type, such as `int`, `float`, `void` (no return), etc.

2. **Function name**: A descriptive name identifying the function.

3. **Parameter list**: Optional inputs the function uses to perform its task. Parameters are specified in parentheses.

4. **Function body**: A block of code (within curly braces `{}`) that performs the task of the function.

Here's the syntax for defining a function:

```cpp
return_type function_name(parameter_list) {
    // Function body
}
```

Example of a Function Definition

Here's a simple function that adds two integers and returns the result:

```cpp
int add(int a, int b) {
    return a + b;  // Return the sum of a and b
}
```

- **Return type**: `int`, because the function returns an integer.

- **Function name**: `add`.

- **Parameter list**: Two integers `a` and `b`.

- **Function body**: It calculates and returns the sum of `a` and `b`.

Calling a Function

To call or invoke a function, you use its name followed by parentheses `()` with arguments if required. When a function is called, control is transferred to the function, which executes its body and then returns control to the calling code, often returning a value.

```cpp
int result = add(5, 10);  // Call the add function
std::cout << "Result: " << result << std::endl;
```

This code calls the `add` function with `5` and `10` as arguments. The function returns `15`, which is stored in the variable `result` and printed to the console.

Function Prototype (or Declaration)

Before you use a function in a program, it must be declared. The function declaration (or prototype) specifies the function's return type, name, and parameters but doesn't include the function body. Function prototypes are usually placed before the `main()` function or in a header file. The function definition comes later.

```cpp
int add(int a, int b);  // Function prototype

int main() {
    int result = add(5, 10);
    std::cout << "Result: " << result << std::endl;
}

int add(int a, int b) {  // Function definition
    return a + b;
}
```

- **Prototype**: `int add(int a, int b);` — It tells the compiler what the function looks like, ensuring it can be used before its actual definition.

Void Functions

A `void` function does not return any value. Instead, it

just performs a task.

```cpp
void greet() {
    std::cout << "Hello, welcome to C++ functions!" << std::endl;
}

int main() {
    greet();  // Call the greet function
    return 0;
}
```

In this case, the `greet()` function prints a message but does not return anything, so its return type is `void`.

Returning Values from Functions

Functions in C++ can return values of any type, and

the type of value they return must match the function's declared return type. If a function is supposed to return a value but does not (or vice versa), a compilation error occurs.

```cpp
float multiply(float x, float y) {
    return x * y;  // Return the product of x and y
}
```

When a function returns a value, you can capture it in the calling code:

```cpp
float product = multiply(3.5, 2.0);  // product = 7.0
```

Recursive Functions

C++ allows functions to call themselves, which is known as recursion. Recursive functions are useful for tasks that can be broken down into smaller, similar sub-tasks, such as calculating factorials or Fibonacci sequences.

```cpp
int factorial(int n) {
    if (n <= 1) {
        return 1;
    } else {
        return n * factorial(n - 1); // Recursive call
    }
}


int main() {
    int num = 5;
    std::cout << "Factorial of " << num << " is " << factorial(num) << std::endl;
    return 0;
}
```

```

In this example, the `factorial()` function calls itself with a reduced argument, until it reaches the base case (`n <= 1`), at which point the recursion stops.

## **2. Function Overloading**

Function overloading is a feature of C++ that allows you to define multiple functions with the same name but different parameter lists. The compiler determines which function to call based on the number and types of arguments provided.

### **Defining Overloaded Functions**

You can overload a function by changing:

1. The number of parameters

2. The types of parameters

3. The order of parameters
```

However, overloading based only on the return type is not allowed.

```cpp
int add(int a, int b) {
    return a + b;
}

float add(float a, float b) {
    return a + b;
}

int add(int a, int b, int c) {
    return a + b + c;
}
```

In the example above, the function `add` is overloaded three times:

1. For adding two integers.

2. For adding two floating-point numbers.

3. For adding three integers.

Calling Overloaded Functions

When calling an overloaded function, the compiler automatically selects the appropriate version based on the arguments you pass.

```cpp
int sum1 = add(10, 20);     // Calls the first version (int, int)

float sum2 = add(3.14f, 1.5f); // Calls the second version (float, float)

int sum3 = add(1, 2, 3);    // Calls the third version (int, int, int)
```

Function overloading makes your code more readable and flexible because you can use the same function name for different operations, rather than creating different names for each variant.

Limitations of Function Overloading

Function overloading relies on differences in parameter lists. However, if the function signatures are too similar, the compiler may struggle to differentiate between them.

For example:

```cpp
void print(int x) {
    std::cout << "Integer: " << x << std::endl;
}

void print(float x) {
    std::cout << "Float: " << x << std::endl;
}
```

If you call `print(4.0)`, the compiler may have trouble deciding whether to call the `int` or `float` version because the literal `4.0` can be interpreted as either.

Default Parameters with Function Overloading

C++ also supports default parameters with overloaded functions. Default parameters are specified in the function prototype or definition, and they allow you to call the function without providing values for all parameters.

```cpp
void display(int x = 10, int y = 20) {
    std::cout << "x = " << x << ", y = " << y << std::endl;
}

int main() {
    display();      // Uses default values: x = 10, y = 20
    display(5);     // Uses default y: x = 5, y = 20
```

    display(5, 15);   // x = 5, y = 15

}
```

---

## **3. Passing Arguments: By Value and By Reference**

In C++, function arguments can be passed in two main ways: **by value** or **by reference**. These methods control how data is passed to functions and whether modifications made to the parameters inside the function affect the original arguments.

### **Passing by Value**

When passing arguments by value, the function receives a copy of the argument's value. Any changes made to the parameter within the function do not affect the original argument in the calling function.

```cpp

```cpp
void incrementByValue(int a) {
    a += 1;
}


int main() {
    int num = 5;
    incrementByValue(num);
    std::cout << "num: " << num << std::endl;  // Output: num: 5 (unchanged)
    return 0;
}
```

In this example, the variable `num` is passed by value to the `incrementByValue` function. Inside the function, `a` is incremented, but this change does not affect `num` in the `main()` function.

Passing by Reference

When passing by reference, the function operates directly on the original argument rather than a copy. This means that any changes made to the parameter within the function affect the original argument in the calling function.

In C++, you pass an argument by reference by using the reference operator (`&`) in the parameter list.

```cpp
void incrementByReference(int &a) {
    a += 1;
}

int main() {
    int num = 5;
    incrementByReference(num);
    std::cout << "num: " << num << std::endl; // Output: num: 6 (changed)
```

        return 0;

}
```


Here, `num` is passed by reference to the `incrementByReference` function. As a result, the change to `a` inside the function also affects `num`.


### **When to Use Pass by Value or Pass by Reference**


- **Pass by value** is ideal when you want to ensure that the original argument is not modified. It is suitable for passing small, simple data types like integers, floating-point numbers, or characters.


- **Pass by reference** is useful when you need to modify the original argument or avoid copying large amounts of data (such as when passing large arrays or objects). It also improves performance by reducing the overhead of copying data.


### **Passing by Reference with `const`**
```

To protect the argument from being modified, even though it is passed by reference, you can use the `const` keyword.

```cpp
void printValue(const int &a) {
    std::cout << "Value: " << a << std::endl;
}

int main() {
    int num = 10;
    printValue(num);  // Output: Value: 10
    return 0;
}
```

In this case, the `const` keyword ensures that `a` cannot be modified within the `printValue` function.

---

4. Template Functions

Template functions in C++ allow you to write generic functions that work with any data type. Instead of writing multiple versions of a function to handle different data types, you can create a template function that operates on various types.

Defining a Template Function

To define a template function, you use the `template` keyword followed by a template parameter list, which specifies the type(s) the function can accept.

```cpp
template <typename T>
T add(T a, T b) {
    return a + b;
}
```

In this example:

- The `template <typename T>` declaration defines a template parameter `T`, which represents any data type.

- The `add` function takes two parameters of type `T` and returns their sum.

Calling a Template Function

When calling a template function, the compiler automatically deduces the type of the arguments and generates the appropriate function.

```cpp
int sum1 = add(10, 20);      // T is deduced as int
float sum2 = add(3.5f, 2.5f);  // T is deduced as float
```

Template functions provide great flexibility, allowing you to write more generic, reusable code.

Multiple Template Parameters

You can also define template functions that accept multiple template parameters.

```cpp
template <typename T1, typename T2>
auto multiply(T1 a, T2 b) -> decltype(a * b) {
    return a * b;
}
```

In this case, the `multiply` function accepts arguments of different types, and the return type is deduced using the `decltype` keyword.

Non-Type Template Parameters

In addition to type parameters, templates can also accept non-type parameters, such as integers.

```cpp
template <typename T, int N>
T arraySum(T (&arr)[N]) {
    T sum = 0;
    for (int i = 0; i < N; ++i) {
        sum += arr[i];
    }
    return sum;
}


int main() {
    int arr[] = {1, 2, 3, 4, 5};
    std::cout << "Sum: " << arraySum(arr) << std::endl;  // Output: Sum: 15
}
```

Here, the template function `arraySum` takes an array of type `T` and size `N` as parameters and calculates the sum of its elements.

Functions in C++ are a powerful mechanism for organizing and structuring code. Understanding how to define and call functions, overload them, and pass arguments efficiently (by value or by reference) is essential for writing modular and reusable code. Template functions further enhance C++'s flexibility by allowing developers to create generic functions that work with different data types, fostering code reuse and type safety. As you continue to explore C++, functions will play a crucial role in your programming journey.

4. Object-Oriented Programming in C++

Object-Oriented Programming (OOP) is a programming paradigm centered around the concept of objects, which represent real-world entities. OOP organizes code in a way that mimics the structure of real-world systems by defining entities (objects) and their interactions. C++ is a powerful object-oriented language that offers robust OOP features, making it ideal for building scalable, modular, and maintainable applications.

In this comprehensive guide, we'll explore the fundamental concepts of OOP in C++, including classes, objects, constructors, destructors, inheritance, polymorphism, abstract classes, and interfaces.

1. Introduction to OOP Concepts

OOP in C++ revolves around several key concepts:

Key Concepts of OOP

1. **Classes and Objects**: A class is a blueprint for creating objects. An object is an instance of a class. A

class defines the properties (attributes) and behaviors (methods) of the object.

2. **Encapsulation**: Encapsulation refers to bundling data (attributes) and functions (methods) that operate on the data within a class. It restricts access to certain details of an object and ensures controlled interaction with an object's data through access control (private, protected, public).

3. **Abstraction**: Abstraction simplifies complex systems by representing essential features without needing to show underlying implementation details. Classes define the interface for interacting with objects while hiding complex internal logic.

4. **Inheritance**: Inheritance allows one class (called a derived class or subclass) to inherit attributes and behaviors from another class (called a base class or superclass). It promotes code reuse and establishes a relationship between classes.

5. **Polymorphism**: Polymorphism enables objects of different classes to be treated as objects of a common base class. It allows functions to behave differently based on the object calling them,

supporting both method overriding and overloading.

Benefits of OOP in C++

- **Modularity**: Classes help break down complex problems into smaller, manageable components.

- **Reusability**: Code can be reused through inheritance and polymorphism.

- **Maintainability**: By organizing code into classes, it becomes easier to manage and modify the codebase.

- **Extensibility**: New features can be added with minimal changes to existing code.

---

2. Classes and Objects

Classes

A class in C++ defines a user-defined data type that holds its own data members (attributes) and member functions (methods). The syntax for defining a class is as follows:

```cpp
class ClassName {
public:
    // Attributes (data members)
    int attribute1;
    float attribute2;

    // Methods (member functions)
    void method1() {
        // Function body
    }

    int method2(int param) {
        // Function body
        return param;
    }
};
```

- **Access Specifiers**: Classes in C++ use access specifiers to control the visibility of data members and member functions:

  - `public`: Members can be accessed from outside the class.

  - `private`: Members can only be accessed from within the class.

  - `protected`: Members can be accessed from within the class and by derived classes.

Objects

An object is an instance of a class. Once a class is defined, you can create objects from it. Here's an example:

```cpp
class Car {
public:
    string model;
    int year;
```

```cpp
    void displayInfo() {
        std::cout << "Model: " << model << ", Year: " << year << std::endl;
    }
};


int main() {
    Car myCar;  // Create an object of the Car class
    myCar.model = "Toyota Corolla";
    myCar.year = 2020;

    myCar.displayInfo();  // Output: Model: Toyota Corolla, Year: 2020

    return 0;
}
```

In this example:

- `Car` is a class with attributes `model` and `year`,

and a method `displayInfo()` to display the car's information.

- `myCar` is an object of the `Car` class.

Member Functions

Member functions (methods) are functions defined inside a class. They can access and manipulate the object's data members. For example:

```cpp
class Rectangle {
private:
    int length;
    int width;

public:
    // Setter methods
    void setLength(int l) {
        length = l;
    }
```

```cpp
    void setWidth(int w) {
        width = w;
    }

    // Getter methods
    int getArea() {
        return length * width;
    }
};

int main() {
    Rectangle rect;
    rect.setLength(5);
    rect.setWidth(10);
    std::cout << "Area: " << rect.getArea() << std::endl;  // Output: Area: 50
    return 0;
}
```

```

In this example, we use setter methods (`setLength()` and `setWidth()`) to assign values to private data members, and a getter method (`getArea()`) to calculate and return the area.

---

## **3. Constructors and Destructors**

### **Constructors**

A constructor is a special member function of a class that is automatically called when an object of the class is created. It initializes the object's data members. The constructor has the same name as the class and does not have a return type.

```cpp
class Person {
public:
    string name;

```cpp
    int age;

    // Constructor
    Person(string personName, int personAge) {
        name = personName;
        age = personAge;
    }

    void displayInfo() {
        std::cout << "Name: " << name << ", Age: " << age << std::endl;
    }
};

int main() {
    Person p1("Alice", 30);
    p1.displayInfo();  // Output: Name: Alice, Age: 30
    return 0;
}
```

```

In this example:

- The constructor `Person(string, int)` initializes the `name` and `age` attributes of the `Person` object when it is created.

- `p1` is initialized with the name "Alice" and age 30 using the constructor.

### **Types of Constructors**

1. **Default Constructor**: A constructor that does not take any parameters. If no constructor is defined, the compiler provides a default constructor.

```cpp
class Animal {
public:
    Animal() {  // Default constructor
        std::cout << "An animal is created!" << std::endl;
    }
};
```
```

```

2. **Parameterized Constructor**: A constructor that takes arguments and initializes an object with specific values.

3. **Copy Constructor**: A constructor that creates a new object as a copy of an existing object.

```cpp
class CopyExample {
public:
    int x;
    CopyExample(int a) : x(a) {}

    // Copy constructor
    CopyExample(const CopyExample &obj) {
        x = obj.x;
    }
};
```
```

```

### **Destructors**

A destructor is a special member function of a class that is automatically called when an object goes out of scope or is explicitly deleted. It is used to free resources allocated by the object. The destructor has the same name as the class but is prefixed with a tilde `~`, and it does not take parameters or return a value.

```cpp
class Resource {
public:
    Resource() {
        std::cout << "Resource acquired" << std::endl;
    }

    ~Resource() {
        std::cout << "Resource released" << std::endl;
    }
};

```cpp
int main() {
    Resource r1;  // Output: Resource acquired
    return 0;     // Output: Resource released
}
```

In this example, the `Resource` class constructor is called when the object `r1` is created, and the destructor is called when the object goes out of scope (at the end of the `main()` function).

---

4. Inheritance and Polymorphism

Inheritance

Inheritance is a mechanism in C++ where one class (derived class) inherits properties and behaviors (data members and methods) from another class (base class). It promotes code reuse and establishes an "is-a" relationship between classes.

```cpp
class Animal {
public:
    void eat() {
        std::cout << "This animal is eating." << std::endl;
    }
};

// Dog class inherits from Animal class
class Dog : public Animal {
public:
    void bark() {
        std::cout << "The dog is barking." << std::endl;
    }
};

int main() {
```

```
    Dog myDog;
    myDog.eat();   // Inherited from Animal class
    myDog.bark();  // Defined in Dog class
    return 0;
}
```

In this example:

- `Animal` is the base class, and `Dog` is the derived class.

- `Dog` inherits the `eat()` method from `Animal` and defines its own method, `bark()`.

Types of Inheritance

1. **Single Inheritance**: A derived class inherits from a single base class.

2. **Multiple Inheritance**: A derived class inherits from more than one base class.

```cpp
```

```cpp
class A {};
class B {};
class C : public A, public B {};
```

3. **Multilevel Inheritance**: A class is derived from a class that is also derived from another class.

```cpp
class A {};
class B : public A {};
class C : public B {};
```

4. **Hierarchical Inheritance**: Multiple classes inherit from the same base class.

```
cpp
```

```
class A {};

class B : public A {};

class C : public A {};
```

Polymorphism

Polymorphism allows objects of different classes to be treated as objects of a common base class. There are two types of polymorphism in C++: **compile-time polymorphism** and **runtime polymorphism**.

Compile-Time Polymorphism (Function Overloading and Operator Overloading)

- **Function Overloading**: Multiple functions with the same name but different parameters can be defined. The appropriate function is called based on the arguments passed.

```cpp
class Calculator {
```

```cpp
public:
    int add(int a, int b) {
        return a + b;
    }

    double add(double a, double b) {
        return a + b;
    }
};
```

- **Operator Overloading**: C++ allows operators to be overloaded so they can work with user-defined types.

```cpp
class Complex {
private:
    int real, imag;
public:
```

```cpp
    Complex(int r = 0, int i = 0) : real(r), imag(i) {}

    // Operator overloading
    Complex operator + (const Complex &obj) {
        return Complex(real + obj.real, imag + obj.imag);
    }
};
```

Runtime Polymorphism (Method Overriding)

Method overriding occurs when a derived class provides a specific implementation of a method that is already defined in its base class. Runtime polymorphism is achieved using **virtual functions** and **pointers** to base class objects.

```cpp
class Animal {
```

```cpp
public:
    virtual void sound() {
        std::cout << "Animal makes a sound." << std::endl;
    }
};


class Dog : public Animal {
public:
    void sound() override {
        std::cout << "Dog barks." << std::endl;
    }
};


int main() {
    Animal *animalPtr;
    Dog d;
    animalPtr = &d;
```

```
    animalPtr->sound();  // Output: Dog barks (runtime polymorphism)

    return 0;
}
```

In this example, the `sound()` method is overridden in the `Dog` class, and a pointer to the base class (`Animal`) is used to call the method at runtime, achieving polymorphism.

---

5. Abstract Classes and Interfaces

Abstract Classes

An **abstract class** in C++ is a class that cannot be instantiated directly. It is designed to be a base class that provides a common interface for derived classes. Abstract classes contain at least one **pure virtual function**, which must be overridden in derived classes.

```cpp
class Shape {
public:
    // Pure virtual function
    virtual void draw() = 0;
};

class Circle : public Shape {
public:
    void draw() override {
        std::cout << "Drawing a circle." << std::endl;
    }
};

class Square : public Shape {
public:
    void draw() override {
        std::cout << "Drawing a square." << std::endl;
```

```cpp
    }
};


int main() {
    Shape *shape1 = new Circle();
    Shape *shape2 = new Square();

    shape1->draw();  // Output: Drawing a circle.
    shape2->draw();  // Output: Drawing a square.

    delete shape1;
    delete shape2;

    return 0;
}
```

In this example, `Shape` is an abstract class with a pure virtual function `draw()`. `Circle` and `Square` are derived classes that override the `draw()` function.

Interfaces in C++

C++ does not have a formal concept of **interfaces** like other programming languages (e.g., Java). However, an interface can be simulated using abstract classes with only pure virtual functions.

```cpp
class InterfaceExample {
public:
    virtual void method1() = 0;
    virtual void method2() = 0;
};
```

In this case, `InterfaceExample` acts as an interface, and any class that inherits from it must implement the `method1()` and `method2()` functions.

Object-Oriented Programming in C++ offers a powerful framework for building complex, modular, and maintainable software systems. Understanding OOP concepts such as classes, objects, inheritance, polymorphism, and abstraction is fundamental for mastering C++ and designing robust applications. These concepts allow developers to model real-world problems effectively and create solutions that are scalable, reusable, and easy to maintain. Whether you're building small applications or large-scale systems, OOP principles will guide you in writing clean, efficient, and modular C++ code.

5. Advanced C++ Features

C++ is a powerful and versatile programming language, and as you move beyond the basics, you'll encounter several advanced features that give you more control over memory management, abstraction, error handling, and performance. These features include pointers and dynamic memory management, smart pointers, templates, and exception handling. In this comprehensive guide, we'll explore these topics in detail and provide examples to illustrate their usage.

---

1. Pointers and Dynamic Memory Management

Pointers

A **pointer** is a variable that stores the memory address of another variable. Pointers are one of the most powerful features of C++ because they provide direct access to memory and enable dynamic memory management, which is crucial for building efficient applications.

Syntax of Pointers

To declare a pointer, use the `*` symbol after the data type. For example:

```cpp
int* ptr; // Pointer to an integer
```

You can assign a pointer the address of a variable using the address-of operator `&` and access the value of the variable pointed to using the dereference operator `*`.

```cpp
int num = 10;
int* ptr = &num; // Pointer storing the address of 'num'
std::cout << "Address of num: " << ptr << std::endl;
std::cout << "Value of num: " << *ptr << std::endl; // Dereferencing the pointer
```

```

**Output**:

```
Address of num: 0x7ffeed02ca14

Value of num: 10
```

### **Pointer Arithmetic**

C++ allows you to perform arithmetic on pointers, which is useful when working with arrays and memory addresses. Common pointer operations include incrementing (`++`), decrementing (`--`), and adding or subtracting integers.

```cpp
int arr[] = {1, 2, 3, 4, 5};
int* ptr = arr;

for (int i = 0; i < 5; ++i) {

```
    std::cout << *ptr << " ";  // Output: 1 2 3 4 5
    ++ptr;
}
```

Here, `ptr` is incremented to traverse the array elements.

Dynamic Memory Management

C++ provides operators `new` and `delete` for dynamic memory management. Dynamic memory allows you to allocate memory during runtime, as opposed to static memory allocation, which occurs at compile-time.

Allocating and Deallocating Memory

- **new operator**: Allocates memory for an object or array.

- **delete operator**: Deallocates memory previously allocated with `new`.

```cpp
int* ptr = new int;  // Dynamically allocate memory for an integer

*ptr = 42;          // Assign a value

std::cout << *ptr << std::endl;  // Output: 42

delete ptr;  // Free the allocated memory
```

You can also allocate arrays dynamically:

```cpp
int* arr = new int[5];  // Dynamically allocate an array of 5 integers

for (int i = 0; i < 5; ++i) {
    arr[i] = i + 1;
}

delete[] arr;  // Deallocate the memory used by the array
```

Dangling Pointers and Memory Leaks

A **dangling pointer** occurs when a pointer continues to point to memory that has been deallocated. This can lead to undefined behavior. To avoid this, set the pointer to `nullptr` after deleting the memory.

```cpp
int* ptr = new int(10);
delete ptr;
ptr = nullptr;  // Safe practice to avoid dangling pointers
```

A **memory leak** occurs when memory is allocated but not properly deallocated. This can happen if you forget to use `delete` after using `new`, leading to wasted memory. Smart pointers, discussed later, help mitigate this issue.

---

2. Smart Pointers

Smart pointers are a feature introduced in C++11 to manage dynamic memory automatically, preventing memory leaks and simplifying memory management. Smart pointers encapsulate raw pointers and ensure proper memory deallocation when the pointer is no longer needed.

C++ provides three main types of smart pointers in the `<memory>` library:

- `std::unique_ptr`
- `std::shared_ptr`
- `std::weak_ptr`

std::unique_ptr

A `std::unique_ptr` represents exclusive ownership of a dynamically allocated object. Only one `unique_ptr` can point to a particular object, and when it goes out of scope, the object is automatically deleted.

Example: Using `std::unique_ptr`

```cpp
#include <iostream>
#include <memory>

class Resource {
public:
    Resource() { std::cout << "Resource acquired" << std::endl; }
    ~Resource() { std::cout << "Resource released" << std::endl; }
};

int main() {
    std::unique_ptr<Resource> res = std::make_unique<Resource>();  // Resource acquired
    return 0;  // Resource released when 'res' goes out of scope
}
```

```

In this example, the `std::unique_ptr` automatically deallocates memory when the object goes out of scope, ensuring that no memory leaks occur.

#### **Transferring Ownership**

Ownership of the object managed by a `std::unique_ptr` can be transferred using `std::move()`.

```cpp
std::unique_ptr<int> ptr1 = std::make_unique<int>(10);

std::unique_ptr<int> ptr2 = std::move(ptr1); // Ownership transferred from ptr1 to ptr2
```

std::shared_ptr

A `std::shared_ptr` allows multiple pointers to share ownership of the same object. The object is deleted when the last `shared_ptr` pointing to it is destroyed
```

or reset. This is done through reference counting.

Example: Using `std::shared_ptr`

```cpp
#include <iostream>
#include <memory>

class Resource {
public:
    Resource() { std::cout << "Resource acquired" << std::endl; }
    ~Resource() { std::cout << "Resource released" << std::endl; }
};

int main() {
    std::shared_ptr<Resource> ptr1 = std::make_shared<Resource>();  // Resource acquired
    {
```

```
    std::shared_ptr<Resource> ptr2 = ptr1;  // Shared ownership

    std::cout << "Resource still owned by two pointers" << std::endl;

  }  // ptr2 goes out of scope, but the resource is still owned by ptr1


  std::cout << "Resource owned by one pointer" << std::endl;

  return 0;  // Resource released when ptr1 goes out of scope
}
```

In this example, `ptr1` and `ptr2` share ownership of the same `Resource` object. The object is deleted only when the last `shared_ptr` (i.e., `ptr1`) is destroyed.

std::weak_ptr

A `std::weak_ptr` is a non-owning smart pointer that references an object managed by a `std::shared_ptr`. It does not affect the reference count of the object and is useful to avoid cyclic references that can lead to memory leaks.

Example: Using `std::weak_ptr`

```cpp
#include <iostream>
#include <memory>

class Resource {
public:
    Resource() { std::cout << "Resource acquired" << std::endl; }
    ~Resource() { std::cout << "Resource released" << std::endl; }
};

int main() {
    std::shared_ptr<Resource> sptr = std::make_shared<Resource>();
    std::weak_ptr<Resource> wptr = sptr;  // Weak
```

reference to the resource

```
    if (std::shared_ptr<Resource> temp = wptr.lock()) {
        std::cout << "Resource is still alive" << std::endl;
    } else {
        std::cout << "Resource has been destroyed" << std::endl;
    }

    return 0;
}
```

Here, `wptr` weakly references the resource managed by `sptr`. The `lock()` method is used to obtain a `shared_ptr` if the resource is still available, or it returns `nullptr` if the resource has been destroyed.

---

3. Templates and Generic Programming

Templates in C++ allow you to write generic code that works with different data types. By using templates, you can create functions and classes that operate on a variety of data types without rewriting the code for each specific type.

Function Templates

A function template defines a pattern for a family of functions. The actual function is instantiated when the compiler encounters a call to the template function.

Defining a Function Template

```cpp
template <typename T>
T add(T a, T b) {
    return a + b;
}
```

```cpp
int main() {
    std::cout << add(10, 20) << std::endl;    // Output: 30 (int)
    std::cout << add(2.5, 3.1) << std::endl;  // Output: 5.6 (double)
    return 0;
}
```

In this example, the `add()` function template can work with both `int` and `double` types.

Class Templates

A class template allows you to create a generic class that works with different data types.

Defining a Class Template

```cpp
template <typename T>
class Box {
private:
    T value;
public:
    Box(T v) : value(v) {}
    T getValue() const {
        return value;
    }
};

int main() {
    Box<int> intBox(10);
    Box<double> doubleBox(3.14);

    std::cout << intBox.getValue() << std::endl;   //
```

Output: 10

    std::cout << doubleBox.getValue() << std::endl; // Output: 3.14

    return 0;
}
```

In this example, `Box` is a generic class that works with different data types like `int` and `double`.

### **Template Specialization**

Template specialization allows you to define a specific implementation of a template for a particular type.

#### **Example: Template Specialization**

```cpp
template <typename T>

```cpp
class Box {
public:
    Box(T v) {
        std::cout << "Generic Box" << std::endl;
    }
};


// Specialization for int type
template <>
class Box<int> {
public:
    Box(int v) {
        std::cout << "Specialized Box for int" << std::endl;
    }
};


int main() {
    Box<double> doubleBox(3.14);   // Output: Generic Box
```

```
    Box<int> intBox(10);        // Output: Specialized Box for int

    return 0;
}
```

In this example, the `Box` template is specialized for `int` type, providing a different implementation than the generic version.

---

4. Exception Handling

Exception handling in C++ provides a way to handle runtime errors and other unexpected situations in a program. It allows you to write code that can recover gracefully from errors without crashing.

Basic Syntax of Exception Handling

C++ uses three keywords for exception handling:

- `try`: Block of code where exceptions may occur.
- `throw`: Used to throw an exception.
- `catch`: Block of code that handles the exception.

Example: Basic Exception Handling

```cpp
#include <iostream>
#include <stdexcept>

int divide(int a, int b) {
    if (b == 0) {
        throw std::runtime_error("Division by zero!");
    }
    return a / b;
}
```

```cpp
int main() {
    try {
        std::cout << divide(10, 0) << std::endl;
    } catch (const std::exception& e) {
        std::cout << "Error: " << e.what() << std::endl;
    }
    return 0;
}
```

Output:

```
Error: Division by zero!
```

In this example, the `divide()` function throws an exception if the divisor is zero. The `catch` block catches the exception and displays the error message.

Throwing Exceptions

Exceptions can be thrown using the `throw` keyword. You can throw any object, but it is common to throw objects of types derived from `std::exception`.

```cpp
void checkPositive(int x) {
    if (x < 0) {
        throw std::invalid_argument("Negative value not allowed");
    }
}
```

Catching Exceptions

Exceptions are caught using the `catch` keyword. You can catch exceptions by value, by reference, or by pointer.

```cpp
```

```cpp
try {
    // Code that might throw an exception
} catch (const std::exception& e) {
    std::cout << "Caught exception: " << e.what() << std::endl;
}
```

Stack Unwinding

When an exception is thrown, C++ performs **stack unwinding**, which means that the destructors of all objects in the scope of the `try` block are called in reverse order before the exception is passed to the `catch` block.

Example: Stack Unwinding

```cpp
class Test {
public:
```

```cpp
    Test() { std::cout << "Constructor called" << std::endl; }

    ~Test() { std::cout << "Destructor called" << std::endl; }
};


int main() {
    try {
        Test t;
        throw std::runtime_error("An error occurred");
    } catch (const std::exception& e) {
        std::cout << "Exception caught: " << e.what() << std::endl;
    }
    return 0;
}
```

Output:
```
```

```
Constructor called
Destructor called
Exception caught: An error occurred
```

Custom Exception Classes

You can define your own exception classes by inheriting from `std::exception` or any of its subclasses.

```cpp
class MyException : public std::exception {
public:
    const char* what() const noexcept override {
        return "Custom exception occurred";
    }
};

int main() {
```

```
    try {
        throw MyException();
    } catch (const std::exception& e) {
        std::cout << e.what() << std::endl;
    }
    return 0;
}
```

Output:

```
Custom exception occurred
```

Conclusion

Advanced features in C++ such as pointers, dynamic

memory management, smart pointers, templates, and exception handling provide powerful tools for building efficient, flexible, and robust applications. Understanding these features allows you to write high-performance code, manage resources effectively, and handle errors gracefully.

- **Pointers** give you low-level control over memory.

- **Smart pointers** automate memory management and prevent memory leaks.

- **Templates** enable generic programming, allowing code reuse for different data types.

- **Exception handling** provides a way to manage errors and exceptional conditions gracefully.

Mastering these advanced features is essential for becoming proficient in C++ and leveraging its full potential in software development.

6. The Standard Template Library

The Standard Template Library (STL) is a powerful set of C++ template classes that provide generic classes and functions for data structures and algorithms. The STL includes a rich collection of containers, iterators, algorithms, and function objects (functors). It enables developers to implement data structures and algorithms without having to write them from scratch, which enhances productivity and code quality. In this guide, we'll explore the STL in detail, covering its components and providing examples to illustrate its use.

---

1. Overview of STL

STL is a library that provides a collection of algorithms and data structures. The key components of the STL include:

- **Containers**: Objects that store data. They include vectors, lists, sets, maps, and more.

- **Iterators**: Objects that provide a way to access elements of containers sequentially without exposing the underlying representation.

- **Algorithms**: Functions that operate on containers and can be used to perform operations like searching, sorting, and modifying data.

- **Function Objects (Functors)**: Objects that can be called as if they were functions, allowing you to encapsulate operations and use them with STL algorithms.

STL promotes code reuse and provides a standardized way to handle common programming tasks. It is designed to work seamlessly with the C++ Standard Library, making it an integral part of modern C++ programming.

---

2. Containers

Containers are the backbone of the STL, providing various ways to store and manipulate data. Below are some of the most commonly used container types in

STL:

Vectors

A **vector** is a dynamic array that can grow and shrink in size. It provides fast access to elements through indexing and is efficient for adding or removing elements at the end.

Example: Using Vectors

```cpp
#include <iostream>
#include <vector>

int main() {
    // Declare and initialize a vector
    std::vector<int> vec = {1, 2, 3, 4, 5};

    // Add elements to the vector
```

```cpp
    vec.push_back(6);
    vec.push_back(7);

    // Access elements using indexing
    std::cout << "Vector elements: ";
    for (size_t i = 0; i < vec.size(); ++i) {
        std::cout << vec[i] << " ";
    }
    std::cout << std::endl;

    // Remove the last element
    vec.pop_back();

    std::cout << "After pop_back: ";
    for (int val : vec) {
        std::cout << val << " ";
    }
    std::cout << std::endl;
```

    return 0;

}
```

**Output**:

```
Vector elements: 1 2 3 4 5 6 7

After pop_back: 1 2 3 4 5 6
```

Lists

A **list** is a doubly linked list that allows for fast insertions and deletions from both ends. It does not provide direct access to elements through indexing.

Example: Using Lists

```cpp
#include <iostream>

```cpp
#include <list>

int main() {
    // Declare and initialize a list
    std::list<int> lst = {10, 20, 30, 40};

    // Add elements to the front and back
    lst.push_front(5);
    lst.push_back(50);

    // Display list elements
    std::cout << "List elements: ";
    for (int val : lst) {
        std::cout << val << " ";
    }
    std::cout << std::endl;

    // Remove an element
    lst.remove(30);
```

```
    std::cout << "After removing 30: ";
    for (int val : lst) {
        std::cout << val << " ";
    }
    std::cout << std::endl;

    return 0;
}
```

Output:

```
List elements: 5 10 20 30 40 50
After removing 30: 5 10 20 40 50
```

Sets

A **set** is a collection of unique elements stored in a specific order. It automatically handles duplicates and provides efficient lookup, insertion, and deletion.

Example: Using Sets

```cpp
#include <iostream>
#include <set>

int main() {
    // Declare and initialize a set
    std::set<int> mySet = {3, 1, 4, 1, 5, 9, 2};

    // Display set elements (automatically sorted)
    std::cout << "Set elements: ";
    for (int val : mySet) {
        std::cout << val << " ";
    }
    std::cout << std::endl;
```

```cpp
    // Add an element
    mySet.insert(6);

    // Remove an element
    mySet.erase(3);

    std::cout << "After modifications: ";
    for (int val : mySet) {
        std::cout << val << " ";
    }
    std::cout << std::endl;

    return 0;
}
```

Output:

```
```

Set elements: 1 2 3 4 5 9

After modifications: 1 2 4 5 6 9

```

### **Maps**

A **map** is a collection of key-value pairs, where each key is unique. Maps allow fast retrieval of values based on keys.

#### **Example: Using Maps**

```cpp
#include <iostream>
#include <map>

int main() {
    // Declare and initialize a map
    std::map<std::string, int> ageMap = {{"Alice", 30}, {"Bob", 25}, {"Charlie", 35}};

```cpp
// Add a key-value pair
ageMap["Dave"] = 40;

// Access and display values
std::cout << "Ages: " << std::endl;
for (const auto& pair : ageMap) {
    std::cout << pair.first << ": " << pair.second << std::endl;
}

// Remove a key-value pair
ageMap.erase("Alice");

std::cout << "After removing Alice: " << std::endl;
for (const auto& pair : ageMap) {
    std::cout << pair.first << ": " << pair.second << std::endl;
}
```

```
    return 0;
}
```

Output:

```
Ages:
Alice: 30
Bob: 25
Charlie: 35
Dave: 40
After removing Alice:
Bob: 25
Charlie: 35
Dave: 40
```

---

3. Iterators and Algorithms

Iterators

Iterators are objects that provide a way to traverse the elements of a container. They can be thought of as generalized pointers that can be used with different container types. STL provides several types of iterators:

- **Input Iterators**: Can read data from a container.

- **Output Iterators**: Can write data to a container.

- **Forward Iterators**: Can read and write data, and can only move forward.

- **Bidirectional Iterators**: Can move both forward and backward.

- **Random Access Iterators**: Can move to any element and support pointer arithmetic.

Example: Using Iterators

```cpp
```

```cpp
#include <iostream>
#include <vector>

int main() {
    std::vector<int> vec = {10, 20, 30, 40, 50};

    // Use iterator to traverse the vector
    std::vector<int>::iterator it;
    std::cout << "Vector elements: ";
    for (it = vec.begin(); it != vec.end(); ++it) {
        std::cout << *it << " ";
    }
    std::cout << std::endl;

    return 0;
}
```

Output:

```
Vector elements: 10 20 30 40 50
```

Algorithms

STL provides a rich set of algorithms that operate on containers using iterators. Common algorithms include:

- **Sorting**: `std::sort()`
- **Searching**: `std::find()`, `std::binary_search()`
- **Transforming**: `std::transform()`
- **Modifying**: `std::for_each()`, `std::remove()`

Example: Using Algorithms

```cpp
#include <iostream>
#include <vector>
```

```cpp
#include <algorithm>

int main() {
    std::vector<int> vec = {5, 2, 3, 1, 4};

    // Sort the vector
    std::sort(vec.begin(), vec.end());

    // Display sorted elements
    std::cout << "Sorted vector: ";
    for (int val : vec) {
        std::cout << val << " ";
    }
    std::cout << std::endl;

    // Find an element
    auto it = std::find(vec.begin(), vec.end(), 3);
    if (it != vec.end()) {
        std::cout << "Element 3 found in the vector." <<
```

```
        std::endl;
    } else {
        std::cout << "Element 3 not found in the vector." << std::endl;
    }

    return 0;
}
```

Output:

```
Sorted vector: 1 2 3 4 5
Element 3 found in the vector.
```

---

4. Function Objects and Lambdas

Function Objects (Functors)

A **function object** or **functor** is an object that can be called as if it were a function. Functors are created by defining a class with an overloaded `operator()`.

Example: Using Function Objects

```cpp
#include <iostream>
#include <vector>
#include <algorithm>

class Add {
public:
    Add(int num) : number(num) {}
    int operator()(int x) const {
```

```cpp
        return x + number;
    }
private:
    int number;
};


int main() {
    std::vector<int> vec = {1, 2, 3, 4, 5};
    std::vector<int> result;

    // Using a functor to add 10 to each element
    std::transform(vec.begin(), vec.end(), std::back_inserter(result), Add(10));

    std::cout << "Resulting vector after adding 10: ";
    for (int val : result) {
        std::cout << val << " ";
    }
    std::cout << std::endl;
```

```
    return 0;
}
```

Output:

```
Resulting vector after adding 10: 11 12 13 14 15
```

Lambda Expressions

Lambda expressions provide a concise way to define anonymous function objects directly in the code. They are particularly useful for passing functions as arguments to algorithms.

Example: Using Lambda Expressions

```cpp
```

```cpp
#include <iostream>
#include <vector>
#include <algorithm>

int main() {
    std::vector<int> vec = {1, 2, 3, 4, 5};

    // Using a lambda to print each element
    std::for_each(vec.begin(), vec.end(), [](int x) {
        std::cout << x << " ";
    });
    std::cout << std::endl;

    // Using a lambda to double each element
    std::transform(vec.begin(), vec.end(), vec.begin(), [](int x) {
        return x * 2;
    });
```

```cpp
    std::cout << "Doubled vector: ";
    for (int val : vec) {
        std::cout << val << " ";
    }
    std::cout << std::endl;

    return 0;
}
```

Output:

```
1 2 3 4 5
Doubled vector: 2 4 6 8 10
```

The Standard Template Library (STL) in C++ is a powerful tool that provides a wide range of data structures, algorithms, and utilities. Understanding STL is essential for writing efficient and effective C+

+ programs. The use of containers such as vectors, lists, sets, and maps, along with iterators and algorithms, can significantly enhance the productivity of developers.

Furthermore, function objects and lambda expressions allow for flexible and reusable code, enabling developers to create more expressive algorithms. By mastering the STL, you can write cleaner, more maintainable code and take full advantage of C++'s capabilities in developing robust applications. The STL is not just a library; it is a way to approach programming problems efficiently and elegantly, making it an invaluable asset for any C++ programmer.

7.File Input/Output in C++

File input and output (I/O) is a critical part of many applications, allowing programs to interact with external files to read data or store results. In C++, the process of working with files is built around the concept of **streams**. Streams provide a consistent way to read and write data, not only to files but also to other input/output devices like the console.

This comprehensive guide covers the essentials of file I/O in C++, including streams, file reading/writing techniques, and error handling in file operations. We'll use numerous examples to demonstrate how to work with files efficiently.

---

1. Working with Streams

In C++, a **stream** is an abstraction that represents a source or destination of data. There are two primary types of streams:

- **Input Streams**: Used for reading data (e.g., reading from a file).

- **Output Streams**: Used for writing data (e.g., writing to a file).

C++ provides several stream classes for file I/O:

- **`ifstream`**: Input stream class to read from files.
- **`ofstream`**: Output stream class to write to files.
- **`fstream`**: Stream class that supports both reading and writing.

These classes are part of the `<fstream>` library, which must be included when working with file I/O.

Basic Stream Operations

Input and Output Streams

The basic stream classes you use for console input/output are `cin` (for reading) and `cout` (for writing). They belong to the iostream library.

```cpp
#include <iostream>

int main() {
    int num;

    // Reading input from console using cin
    std::cout << "Enter a number: ";
    std::cin >> num;

    // Writing output to console using cout
    std::cout << "You entered: " << num << std::endl;

    return 0;
}
```

Output:

```
Enter a number: 42
You entered: 42
```

In the context of file I/O, `ifstream`, `ofstream`, and `fstream` serve a similar role as `cin` and `cout`, but they operate on files instead of the console.

Types of Streams

- **`ifstream` (Input File Stream)**: This class is used to open a file for reading. The input can be read from the file using this stream.

- **`ofstream` (Output File Stream)**: This class is used to open a file for writing. You can write output to the file using this stream.

- **`fstream` (File Stream)**: This class allows both reading and writing from/to a file. It combines the functionality of `ifstream` and `ofstream`.

Example: Opening a File for Reading and Writing

Here's how you can open a file for reading and writing using `fstream`:

```cpp
#include <iostream>
#include <fstream>

int main() {
    // Create a file stream object
    std::fstream file;

    // Open the file in read-write mode
    file.open("example.txt", std::ios::in | std::ios::out | std::ios::app);
```

```cpp
    if (!file) {
        std::cerr << "File could not be opened!" << std::endl;
        return 1;
    }

    // Write some data to the file
    file << "Hello, World!" << std::endl;

    // Read data from the file (rewind to the beginning first)
    file.seekg(0);
    std::string line;
    while (std::getline(file, line)) {
        std::cout << line << std::endl;
    }

    // Close the file
    file.close();
```

```
    return 0;
}
```

---

2. Reading from and Writing to Files

Writing to Files

Writing to a file in C++ is done using the `ofstream` class. You need to specify the filename and the mode in which the file should be opened. There are multiple modes you can use:

- **`std::ios::out`**: Opens a file for writing. If the file exists, its content is deleted.

- **`std::ios::app`**: Opens a file for appending. If the file exists, data is added to the end of the file without modifying existing data.

Example: Writing to a File Using ofstream

```cpp
#include <iostream>
#include <fstream>

int main() {
    // Create an ofstream object for writing to a file
    std::ofstream outFile;

    // Open the file in write mode
    outFile.open("output.txt");

    // Check if the file is open
    if (outFile.is_open()) {
        // Write data to the file
        outFile << "This is a line of text.\n";
        outFile << "This is another line of text.\n";
```

```
    // Close the file
    outFile.close();

    std::cout << "Data written to the file successfully." << std::endl;

  } else {

    std::cerr << "Error opening the file for writing." << std::endl;

  }


  return 0;
}
```

In this example, we write two lines of text to `output.txt`. If the file does not exist, it will be created. If the file already exists, its previous content will be overwritten.

Reading from Files

Reading from a file is done using the `ifstream` class.

You can use various methods to read the content, including:

- **`getline()`**: Reads an entire line from the file.
- **`operator>>`**: Reads a word or token from the file.
- **`read()`**: Reads binary data from the file.

Example: Reading from a File Using ifstream

```cpp
#include <iostream>
#include <fstream>
#include <string>

int main() {
    // Create an ifstream object for reading from a file
    std::ifstream inFile;
```

```cpp
// Open the file in read mode
inFile.open("input.txt");

// Check if the file is open
if (inFile.is_open()) {
    std::string line;

    // Read data from the file line by line
    while (std::getline(inFile, line)) {
        std::cout << line << std::endl;
    }

    // Close the file
    inFile.close();
} else {
    std::cerr << "Error opening the file for reading." << std::endl;
}
```

```
    return 0;

}
```

In this example, we read the contents of `input.txt` line by line using `std::getline()` and print it to the console.

Modes for Opening Files

When working with files, you can specify the mode in which the file should be opened. Some common modes are:

- **`std::ios::in`**: Opens the file for reading.

- **`std::ios::out`**: Opens the file for writing.

- **`std::ios::app`**: Opens the file for appending. Data is written at the end of the file.

- **`std::ios::binary`**: Opens the file in binary mode.

- **`std::ios::ate`**: Opens the file and moves the file pointer to the end.

Example: Opening a File in Binary Mode

```cpp
#include <iostream>
#include <fstream>

int main() {
    // Open a binary file for writing
    std::ofstream binFile("binaryfile.dat", std::ios::out | std::ios::binary);

    if (binFile.is_open()) {
        int number = 42;

        // Write the integer to the binary file
        binFile.write(reinterpret_cast<char*>(&number), sizeof(number));

        binFile.close();
```

```cpp
    } else {
        std::cerr << "Error opening binary file." << std::endl;
    }


    // Open the binary file for reading
    std::ifstream binFileIn("binaryfile.dat", std::ios::in | std::ios::binary);


    if (binFileIn.is_open()) {
        int numberRead;


        // Read the integer from the binary file
binFileIn.read(reinterpret_cast<char*>(&numberRead), sizeof(numberRead));


        std::cout << "Number read from binary file: " << numberRead << std::endl;
        binFileIn.close();
    } else {
```

```
        std::cerr << "Error opening binary file for reading." << std::endl;
    }

    return 0;
}
```

This example demonstrates how to write and read binary data using the `write()` and `read()` functions, which are used with binary files.

---

3. Error Handling in File Operations

Error handling is a crucial part of file I/O operations. Files might not open correctly for several reasons, such as the file not existing, permissions being denied, or the disk being full. C++ provides various mechanisms to handle such errors gracefully.

Checking File Status

C++ provides several functions to check the status of a file stream:

- **`is_open()`**: Checks if a file stream is successfully opened.
- **`good()`**: Returns `true` if the stream is in a good state.
- **`fail()`**: Returns `true` if an error occurred in an I/O operation.
- **`bad()`**: Returns `true` if a non-recoverable error occurred.
- **`eof()`**: Returns `true` if the end of the file is reached.

Example: Error Handling in File Operations

```cpp
#include <iostream>
#include <fstream>
```

```cpp
int main() {
    // Attempt to open a file for reading
    std::ifstream file("nonexistent.txt");

    // Check if the file was opened successfully
    if (!file.is_open()) {
        std::cerr << "Error: Could not open file!" << std::endl;
        return 1;
    }

    // Check if the file stream is in a good state
    if (file.good()) {
        std::string line;
        while (std::getline(file, line)) {
            std::cout << line << std::endl;
```

        }
    }

   // Check if the end of the file was reached
   if (file.eof()) {
       std::cout << "Reached the end of the file." << std::endl;
   }

   // Check if a fail occurred (e.g., trying to read an integer from a string)
   if (file.fail()) {
       std::cerr << "Error: A fail occurred in file operations!" << std::endl;
   }

   // Close the file
   file.close();

   return 0;

```
}
```

In this example, we attempt to open a file that doesn't exist, handle the error, and check various file states (e.g., `good()`, `eof()`, and `fail()`).

Exceptions for File I/O

C++ allows you to use exceptions to handle errors in file operations. You can enable exceptions on file streams by calling the `exceptions()` method and then catch the exception using `try-catch` blocks.

Example: Using Exceptions for Error Handling

```cpp
#include <iostream>
#include <fstream>
```

```cpp
int main() {
    std::ifstream file;

    try {
        // Enable exceptions on the file stream
        file.exceptions(std::ifstream::failbit | std::ifstream::badbit);

        // Open the file
        file.open("nonexistent.txt");

        // Attempt to read from the file
        std::string line;
        while (std::getline(file, line)) {
            std::cout << line << std::endl;
        }
    } catch (const std::ios_base::failure& e) {
        std::cerr << "File error: " << e.what() << std::endl;
    }
```

```
    return 0;
}
```

In this example, exceptions are enabled for file operations, and any I/O failure will trigger the exception, which we handle in the `catch` block.

File input/output in C++ is an essential skill for reading from and writing to files. By understanding the stream classes (`ifstream`, `ofstream`, and `fstream`), you can easily perform file operations like reading, writing, and even handling errors. Effective error handling, whether through return value checking or exceptions, ensures that your file operations are robust and can handle unexpected conditions gracefully.

Incorporating file I/O into your programs allows you to persist data, making your applications more dynamic and capable of working with large sets of data that exist outside the program's runtime memory. With these foundational skills, you are well-equipped to handle file operations in a variety of C++

applications.

8. Multithreading and Concurrency in C++

Concurrency and multithreading are fundamental concepts in modern programming, allowing developers to write programs that perform multiple tasks simultaneously. This is especially important in the era of multi-core processors, where utilizing multiple threads can significantly boost performance and responsiveness. C++ offers robust support for multithreading, allowing developers to create concurrent programs that execute multiple threads in parallel.

This guide will explore multithreading and concurrency in C++, covering key topics such as threads, thread synchronization, mutexes, locks, futures, and promises. Through examples, we'll demonstrate how to create, manage, and synchronize threads to develop efficient and safe multithreaded applications.

---

1. Introduction to Threads

A **thread** is a sequence of instructions that can be executed independently of other threads. In the context of a program, multithreading allows multiple threads to execute concurrently, sharing the same memory space but performing different tasks. This is distinct from multiprocessing, where multiple processes with separate memory spaces run concurrently.

In C++, multithreading is supported through the `<thread>` library, which provides tools for creating and managing threads.

Creating and Running Threads

To create a thread in C++, you can instantiate an object of the `std::thread` class and pass a function (or a callable object) that the thread should execute.

Example: Creating and Running a Thread

```cpp
#include <iostream>
```

```cpp
#include <thread>

// Function to be executed by the thread
void printMessage() {
    std::cout << "Hello from the thread!" << std::endl;
}

int main() {
    // Create a thread and run the printMessage function
    std::thread t(printMessage);

    // Wait for the thread to finish execution
    t.join();

    std::cout << "Thread execution finished." << std::endl;

    return 0;
}
```

```

**Output**:

```
Hello from the thread!

Thread execution finished.
```

In this example:

- A thread `t` is created, and the function `printMessage` is executed in that thread.

- The `join()` function is used to block the main thread until the new thread finishes execution. Without `join()`, the program might terminate before the thread completes its task.

### **Thread Management**

C++ offers several functions for managing threads:

- **`join()`**: Blocks the current thread until the thread on which it was called finishes execution.
```

- **`detach()`**: Allows the thread to run independently, without waiting for it to finish.

Example: Using `detach()`

```cpp
#include <iostream>
#include <thread>
#include <chrono>

// Function that simulates a long-running task
void longTask() {
    std::this_thread::sleep_for(std::chrono::seconds(5));
    std::cout << "Long task finished." << std::endl;
}

int main() {
    std::thread t(longTask);
```

```
    // Detach the thread to let it run independently
    t.detach();

    std::cout << "Main thread is free to continue." << std::endl;

    // Give enough time for the detached thread to complete
    std::this_thread::sleep_for(std::chrono::seconds(6));

    return 0;
}
```

Output:

```
Main thread is free to continue.
Long task finished.
```

Here, the `detach()` function allows the thread `t` to run independently of the main thread. The main thread continues executing without waiting for `t` to complete, and the long-running task finishes in the background.

---

2. Thread Synchronization

When multiple threads access shared resources (such as variables, files, or data structures), you must ensure that they do not interfere with each other. This is known as **thread synchronization**. Without proper synchronization, data races and undefined behavior can occur, where threads modify shared resources in unpredictable ways.

Data Races

A **data race** occurs when:

1. Two or more threads concurrently access the same memory location.

2. At least one thread modifies the data.

3. No synchronization mechanisms (like locks or atomic operations) are in place to coordinate access.

To avoid data races, C++ provides several synchronization mechanisms, such as **mutexes**, **locks**, and **atomic operations**.

Example: Data Race

```cpp
#include <iostream>
#include <thread>

int counter = 0;

void increment() {
    for (int i = 0; i < 10000; ++i) {
        ++counter;  // Incrementing shared resource
    }
```

```
}


int main() {

    std::thread t1(increment);

    std::thread t2(increment);


    t1.join();

    t2.join();


    std::cout << "Final counter value: " << counter << std::endl;


    return 0;

}
```

In this example, two threads (`t1` and `t2`) both increment the shared `counter` variable. The program might produce an incorrect result due to a data race, as both threads attempt to modify `counter` without synchronization. The output can vary each time the program runs.

Output (example):

```
Final counter value: 13455
```

Here, the expected value is `20000`, but due to a data race, the output is incorrect.

---

3. Mutexes and Locks

A **mutex** (short for "mutual exclusion") is a synchronization primitive that ensures that only one thread can access a critical section of code at a time. By locking a mutex before accessing shared resources, you can prevent data races and ensure thread safety.

C++ provides the `std::mutex` class to manage mutexes.

Using Mutex for Thread Safety

To fix the data race in the previous example, we can use a mutex to synchronize access to the `counter` variable.

Example: Using Mutex for Synchronization

```cpp
#include <iostream>
#include <thread>
#include <mutex>

int counter = 0;
std::mutex mtx;

void increment() {
```

```cpp
    for (int i = 0; i < 10000; ++i) {
        std::lock_guard<std::mutex> lock(mtx);  // Lock the mutex
        ++counter;
    }
}

int main() {
    std::thread t1(increment);
    std::thread t2(increment);

    t1.join();
    t2.join();

    std::cout << "Final counter value: " << counter << std::endl;

    return 0;
}
```
```
```

Output:

```
Final counter value: 20000
```

In this example:

- The `std::lock_guard` object locks the mutex `mtx` when it is created and automatically unlocks it when it goes out of scope.

- The critical section (incrementing `counter`) is protected by the mutex, ensuring that only one thread can access it at a time, preventing a data race.

Deadlocks

A **deadlock** occurs when two or more threads are blocked, each waiting for a resource held by another thread. Deadlocks can arise when multiple threads attempt to lock multiple mutexes in different orders.

Example: Deadlock Scenario

```cpp
#include <iostream>
#include <thread>
#include <mutex>

std::mutex mtx1, mtx2;

void thread1() {
    std::lock_guard<std::mutex> lock1(mtx1);

std::this_thread::sleep_for(std::chrono::milliseconds(10));  // Simulate work
    std::lock_guard<std::mutex> lock2(mtx2);
    std::cout << "Thread 1 finished." << std::endl;
}

void thread2() {
    std::lock_guard<std::mutex> lock2(mtx2);
```

```cpp
    std::this_thread::sleep_for(std::chrono::milliseconds(10));  // Simulate work
    std::lock_guard<std::mutex> lock1(mtx1);
    std::cout << "Thread 2 finished." << std::endl;
}


int main() {
    std::thread t1(thread1);
    std::thread t2(thread2);

    t1.join();
    t2.join();

    return 0;
}
```

In this example, `thread1` locks `mtx1` first, while `thread2` locks `mtx2` first. Each thread then tries to lock the other mutex, leading to a deadlock where both threads are blocked, waiting for each other indefinitely.

Avoiding Deadlocks

One way to avoid deadlocks is by ensuring that all threads lock mutexes in the same order. Alternatively, you can use `std::lock()`, which locks multiple mutexes without risk of deadlocks.

Example: Avoiding Deadlock with `std::lock()`

```cpp
#include <iostream>
#include <thread>
#include <mutex>

std::mutex mtx1, mtx2;

void thread1() {
```

```cpp
    std::lock(mtx1, mtx2);  // Lock both mutexes without risk of deadlock

    std::lock_guard<std::mutex> lock1(mtx1, std::adopt_lock);

    std::lock_guard<std::mutex> lock2(mtx2, std::adopt_lock);

    std::cout << "Thread 1 finished." << std::endl;
}


void thread2() {

    std::lock(mtx1, mtx2);  // Lock both mutexes without risk of deadlock

    std::lock_guard<std::mutex> lock2(mtx2, std::adopt_lock);

    std::lock_guard<std::mutex> lock1(mtx1, std::adopt_lock);

    std::cout << "Thread 2 finished." << std::endl;
}


int main() {

    std::thread t
```

```
1(thread1);
    std::thread t2(thread2);

    t1.join();
    t2.join();

    return 0;
}
```

In this example, `std::lock()` ensures that both mutexes are locked without risk of deadlock, regardless of the order in which they are locked.

---

4. Futures and Promises

In addition to mutexes and locks, C++ provides

higher-level abstractions for managing multithreaded code, such as **futures** and **promises**. These are particularly useful for managing the results of asynchronous tasks, ensuring that threads can return values or signal completion in a safe and synchronized manner.

Futures

A **future** is an object that represents the result of an asynchronous operation. The result may not be immediately available, but the future provides a mechanism to wait for it. You can obtain a future using `std::async` or in combination with a promise.

Example: Using `std::async` and `std::future`

```cpp
#include <iostream>
#include <future>
#include <chrono>
```

```cpp
// Function to perform a long computation
int longComputation() {
    std::this_thread::sleep_for(std::chrono::seconds(2)); // Simulate work
    return 42;
}


int main() {
    // Run longComputation asynchronously and get a future
    std::future<int> result = std::async(std::launch::async, longComputation);


    // Do other work while the computation runs
    std::cout << "Doing other work..." << std::endl;


    // Wait for the result and print it
    std::cout << "Result of computation: " << result.get() << std::endl;
```

```
    return 0;
}
```

In this example, `std::async` launches the `longComputation` function asynchronously, returning a `std::future` object. The main thread can continue doing other work, and when the result is needed, `result.get()` blocks until the computation finishes.

Promises

A **promise** is an object used to set a value that will be returned by a future. The promise provides the mechanism to set the value, while the future is used to retrieve it. This is useful for passing results between threads.

Example: Using `std::promise` and `std::future`

```cpp
```

```cpp
#include <iostream>
#include <thread>
#include <future>

// Function that computes a result and sets the promise
void computeResult(std::promise<int> p) {
    std::this_thread::sleep_for(std::chrono::seconds(2)); // Simulate work
    p.set_value(42);  // Set the result in the promise
}

int main() {
    // Create a promise and its associated future
    std::promise<int> p;
    std::future<int> result = p.get_future();

    // Launch a thread to perform the computation
    std::thread t(computeResult, std::move(p));
```

```cpp
    // Wait for the result and print it
    std::cout << "Result of computation: " << result.get() << std::endl;

    t.join();

    return 0;
}
```

In this example, a `std::promise` is used to set the result of the computation in one thread, while the main thread waits for the result using the associated `std::future`.

Multithreading and concurrency in C++ are powerful tools for building high-performance, responsive applications that can take advantage of modern multi-core processors. Through threads, mutexes, locks, futures, and promises, C++ provides a comprehensive set of features to manage concurrent tasks efficiently and safely.

By understanding and applying these concepts—such as thread creation, synchronization using mutexes and locks, and the use of futures and promises—you can write robust multithreaded applications that perform complex operations in parallel, significantly improving the performance and responsiveness of your programs. However, it is also important to handle potential pitfalls, such as data races and deadlocks, ensuring that multithreaded code is both efficient and safe.

9. Best Practices and Design Patterns in C++

C++ is a complex and versatile language that allows developers to create high-performance, system-level software, but it also poses challenges when it comes to writing clean, maintainable, and efficient code. Following best practices, coding standards, and leveraging design patterns can significantly improve the quality of your C++ programs.

This guide explores essential best practices for C++ development, including coding standards, common design patterns, performance optimization techniques, unit testing, and more. The appendices provide additional resources, including a C++ language reference, useful libraries, and common errors with debugging tips.

1. Coding Standards and Style Guidelines

Adhering to coding standards and guidelines ensures consistency, readability, and maintainability across a codebase, especially in large teams or projects. C++ does not have a single universally accepted coding standard, but there are several widely adopted guidelines, such as those from Google, LLVM, and the ISO C++ Core Guidelines.

Naming Conventions

1. **Variables and Functions**: Use descriptive names for variables and functions, following a consistent naming convention. A common convention in C++ is **camelCase** or **snake_case** for variable names and **PascalCase** for class names.

   - Example:

   ```cpp
   int employeeId;
   std::string employeeName;
   void calculateSalary();
   ```

2. **Constants**: Use **ALL_CAPS** with underscores for constants.

   - Example:

   ```cpp
   const int MAX_SIZE = 100;
   ```

3. **Class Names**: Class names should be in **PascalCase** (also known as UpperCamelCase).

   - Example:

   ```cpp
   class EmployeeDetails {
       // Class members...
   };
   ```

4. **Member Variables**: Use a prefix like `m_` to differentiate member variables from local variables.

   - Example:

   ```cpp
   class Person {
       int m_age;
       std::string m_name;
   };
   ```

Formatting

1. **Indentation**: Use consistent indentation, typically 4 spaces per level (avoid tabs). This improves code readability.

   - Example:

   ```cpp
   if (condition) {
       // Indented block of code
       doSomething();
   }
   ```

2. **Braces**: Place opening braces on the same line as the control structure, following the **K&R style** or **Allman style**. K&R is more common in C++.

   - Example (K&R):

   ```cpp
   if (condition) {
       doSomething();
   ```

```
    } else {
        doSomethingElse();
    }
```

3. **Line Length**: Limit the line length to 80 or 100 characters to improve readability, especially when working with multiple editors or tools.

Commenting and Documentation

1. **Inline Comments**: Use inline comments sparingly and only when necessary to clarify complex code.
   - Example:
   ```cpp
   // Check if the employee is eligible for a bonus
   if (employee.isEligible()) {
       giveBonus();
   }
   ```

```

2. **Function Documentation**: Document each function with comments explaining its purpose, parameters, and return value.

   - Example:

   ```cpp
   // Calculates the annual salary of an employee
   // @param baseSalary - The base monthly salary
   // @param monthsWorked - Number of months worked in the year
   // @return Annual salary based on months worked
   double calculateAnnualSalary(double baseSalary, int monthsWorked) {
       return baseSalary * monthsWorked;
   }
   ```

3. **Doxygen**: Use Doxygen-style comments (`/** */`) to generate documentation from code.

   - Example:

   ```cpp

```
/**
 * @brief Calculates the annual salary of an employee.
 * @param baseSalary The base salary.
 * @param monthsWorked The number of months worked in the year.
 * @return The total annual salary.
 */
double calculateAnnualSalary(double baseSalary, int monthsWorked);
```

Error Handling and Resource Management

1. **RAII (Resource Acquisition Is Initialization)**: Manage resources like memory, file handles, or database connections using RAII. This ensures that resources are automatically released when objects go out of scope.

   - Example:

   ```cpp
   std::ifstream file("example.txt");
   ```

```
    if (!file.is_open()) {
        std::cerr << "Error: Could not open file" << std::endl;
        return;
    }
```

2. **Use Smart Pointers**: Avoid manual memory management with raw pointers. Use `std::unique_ptr` and `std::shared_ptr` for automatic memory management.

   - Example:

   ```cpp
   std::unique_ptr<MyClass> obj = std::make_unique<MyClass>();
   ```

Code Readability and Maintainability

1. **Keep Functions Short**: Each function should perform a single task. Long functions are harder to understand and maintain.

2. **Avoid Global Variables**: Global variables lead to coupling and unexpected side effects. Minimize their use and prefer encapsulation within classes.

3. **Modularize Code**: Split code into smaller, reusable components to improve readability and maintainability.

2. Common Design Patterns in C++

Design patterns are proven solutions to common problems in software design. In C++, these patterns are used to create flexible, reusable, and maintainable code. Below are some of the most commonly used design patterns in C++:

Singleton Pattern

The **Singleton Pattern** ensures that a class has only one instance and provides a global point of access to it.

Example: Singleton Pattern

```cpp
```

```cpp
class Singleton {
private:
    static Singleton* instance;

    // Private constructor to prevent instantiation
    Singleton() {}

public:
    // Public method to get the single instance of the class
    static Singleton* getInstance() {
        if (!instance) {
            instance = new Singleton();
        }
        return instance;
    }
};

// Initialize the static member
```

```cpp
Singleton* Singleton::instance = nullptr;
```

In this pattern, the constructor is private, ensuring that objects cannot be created outside the class. The `getInstance()` function ensures only one instance is created.

Factory Pattern

The **Factory Pattern** provides an interface for creating objects but allows subclasses to alter the type of objects that will be created.

Example: Factory Pattern

```cpp
class Product {
public:
    virtual void use() = 0;
};
```

```cpp
class ConcreteProductA : public Product {
public:
    void use() override {
        std::cout << "Using Product A" << std::endl;
    }
};


class ConcreteProductB : public Product {
public:
    void use() override {
        std::cout << "Using Product B" << std::endl;
    }
};


class ProductFactory {
public:
    static Product* createProduct(const std::string& type) {
```

```cpp
        if (type == "A") {
            return new ConcreteProductA();
        } else if (type == "B") {
            return new ConcreteProductB();
        }
        return nullptr;
    }
};
```

The `ProductFactory` class creates instances of `ConcreteProductA` or `ConcreteProductB` based on input.

Observer Pattern

The **Observer Pattern** defines a one-to-many relationship where one object (the **Subject**) notifies a set of objects (**Observers**) when its state changes.

Example: Observer Pattern

```cpp
#include <iostream>
#include <vector>

class Observer {
public:
    virtual void update() = 0;
};

class Subject {
    std::vector<Observer*> observers;

public:
    void addObserver(Observer* observer) {
        observers.push_back(observer);
    }

    void notify() {
```

```cpp
        for (Observer* observer : observers) {
            observer->update();
        }
    }
};


class ConcreteObserver : public Observer {
public:
    void update() override {
        std::cout << "Observer updated!" << std::endl;
    }
};


int main() {
    Subject subject;
    ConcreteObserver observer1, observer2;

    subject.addObserver(&observer1);
    subject.addObserver(&observer2);
```

```
    subject.notify(); // All observers get notified
}
```

In this pattern, the `Subject` maintains a list of observers and notifies them when a change occurs.

Decorator Pattern

The **Decorator Pattern** allows for dynamically adding behavior to an object at runtime without affecting the behavior of other objects from the same class.

Example: Decorator Pattern

```cpp
class Coffee {
public:
```

```cpp
    virtual double cost() const = 0;
    virtual ~Coffee() {}
};


class SimpleCoffee : public Coffee {
public:
    double cost() const override {
        return 2.0;
    }
};


class CoffeeDecorator : public Coffee {
protected:
    Coffee* coffee;
public:
    CoffeeDecorator(Coffee* coffee) : coffee(coffee) {}
};
```

```cpp
class MilkDecorator : public CoffeeDecorator {
public:
    MilkDecorator(Coffee* coffee) : CoffeeDecorator(coffee) {}

    double cost() const override {
        return coffee->cost() + 0.5;
    }
};

int main() {
    Coffee* myCoffee = new SimpleCoffee();
    myCoffee = new MilkDecorator(myCoffee);

    std::cout << "Cost of coffee with milk: $" << myCoffee->cost() << std::endl;
}
```

Here, the `MilkDecorator` adds functionality

(increased cost) to the `SimpleCoffee` class dynamically.

---

3. Performance Optimization Techniques

Optimizing the performance of C++ code is crucial for building high-performance applications. Below are some common techniques for improving performance:

1. Avoiding Unnecessary Copies

Minimize the number of object copies in your code by using **move semantics**. C++11 introduced **rvalue references** and the **move constructor** to optimize performance when an object is moved rather than copied.

Example: Move Semantics

```cpp
class MyClass {
public:
    MyClass() {}

    // Copy constructor
    MyClass(const MyClass& other) {
        std::cout << "Copy constructor called!" << std::endl;
    }

    // Move constructor
    MyClass(MyClass&& other) noexcept {
        std::cout << "Move constructor called!" << std::endl;
    }
};

int main() {
```

```
MyClass obj1;

MyClass obj2 = std::move(obj1);  // Move instead of copy
}
```

2. Using `const` Correctly

Mark variables, function parameters, and methods as `const` whenever possible. This allows the compiler to optimize code better and prevents unintended modifications.

3. Reserve Space in Containers

When working with containers like `std::vector`, use the `reserve()` function to preallocate memory. This prevents the container from reallocating memory multiple times as new elements are added.

Example: Reserving Space in a Vector

```cpp
```

```cpp
std::vector<int> numbers;
numbers.reserve(100);  // Preallocate space for 100 elements
for (int i = 0; i < 100; ++i) {
    numbers.push_back(i);
}
```

4. Inlining Small Functions

Use the `inline` keyword for small functions to avoid the overhead of a function call.

Example: Inline Function

```cpp
inline int add(int a, int b) {
    return a + b;
}
```

5. Profile and Measure Performance

Use profiling tools like **gprof**, **Valgrind**, or IDE-integrated profilers to identify bottlenecks in your code.

---

4. Unit Testing in C++

Unit testing ensures that individual components of a program work correctly. In C++, frameworks like **Google Test (GTest)** and **Catch2** make it easier to write and run unit tests.

Example: Unit Testing with Google Test

```cpp
#include <gtest/gtest.h>
```

```cpp
// Function to test
int add(int a, int b) {
    return a + b;
}
// Unit test
TEST(AdditionTest, PositiveNumbers) {
    EXPECT_EQ(add(1, 2), 3);
}


int main(int argc, char **argv) {
    ::testing::InitGoogleTest(&argc, argv);
    return RUN_ALL_TESTS();
}
```

In this example, the `EXPECT_EQ()` macro compares the result of the `add()` function to the expected value.

Test Driven Development (TDD)

Test Driven Development is a software development practice where tests are written before writing the actual code. This encourages better design and ensures that code is thoroughly tested.

Appendices

Appendix A: C++ Language Reference

This appendix provides a quick reference for common C++ syntax and features, including data types, operators, and control structures.

Appendix B: Useful Libraries

This section lists popular C++ libraries:

1. **Boost**: A large collection of high-quality

libraries that extend the functionality of C++.

2. **Poco**: Provides libraries for networking, file handling, and concurrency.

3. **Eigen**: A popular library for linear algebra and matrix computations.

Appendix C: Common Errors and Debugging Tips

This appendix provides solutions for common C++ errors:

1. **Segmentation Fault**: Usually caused by accessing invalid memory, such as dereferencing a null pointer.

2. **Memory Leaks**: Use smart pointers (`std::unique_ptr`, `std::shared_ptr`) or tools like **Valgrind** to detect and fix memory leaks.

3. **Uninitialized Variables**: Always initialize variables to avoid undefined behavior.

By following best practices, using design patterns, and applying performance optimization techniques, you can write more efficient, maintainable, and scalable C++ applications. Unit testing ensures code correctness and reliability, and a thorough understanding of common errors helps improve debugging skills.

10. C++ Glossary

The C++ programming language is rich in terminology, concepts, and features. This glossary provides definitions for key C++ terms, covering topics from basic syntax and language constructs to advanced programming concepts like object-oriented design, memory management, and concurrency.

A

- **Abstract Class**: A class that cannot be instantiated on its own and is meant to serve as a base class for other classes. It typically contains at least one pure virtual function.
  - Example:
    ```cpp
    class Shape {
    public:
        virtual void draw() = 0; // Pure virtual function
    ```

    };
    ```


- **Access Specifiers**: Keywords (`public`, `protected`, `private`) used to define the visibility and access control of class members.

  - Example:

    ```cpp
    class MyClass {
    private:
        int privateVariable;  // Accessible only within the class
    public:
        int publicVariable;   // Accessible anywhere
    };
    ```


- **Algorithm**: A sequence of steps or rules for performing tasks or solving problems. In C++, many algorithms are provided by the **Standard Template Library (STL)**.
    ```

- **Array**: A collection of elements of the same type stored in contiguous memory locations. C++ supports both static arrays (fixed size) and dynamic arrays (managed by pointers or container classes like `std::vector`).

  - Example:

    ```cpp
    int arr[5] = {1, 2, 3, 4, 5}; // Static array
    ```

- **Argument**: A value passed to a function when it is called. Arguments are used as input to perform a specific operation inside the function.

  - Example:

    ```cpp
    void printNumber(int n) {
        std::cout << n << std::endl;
    }
    printNumber(5); // 5 is an argument
    ```

- **Asynchronous**: A form of programming where tasks are executed independently of the main program flow, often in separate threads or processes. This allows programs to perform tasks concurrently, such as reading from a file while continuing other computations.

  - Example: Use of `std::async` to run a function asynchronously.

B

- **Binary Operator**: An operator that operates on two operands. Examples include `+`, `-`, `*`, `/`, and `==`.

  - Example:

    ```cpp
    int sum = 5 + 3;  // '+' is a binary operator
    ```

- **Bitwise Operators**: Operators that perform operations on the binary representations of integers. Common bitwise operators include `&` (AND), `|` (OR), `^` (XOR), `~` (NOT), `<<` (left shift), and `>>` (right shift).

  - Example:

    ```cpp
    int a = 5; // Binary: 0101
    int b = 3; // Binary: 0011
    int c = a & b; // Result: 0001 (1 in decimal)
    ```

- **Block Scope**: The region of a program within curly braces `{}` where variables are visible. Variables declared in a block scope are only accessible within that block.

  - Example:

    ```cpp
    if (condition) {
        int x = 5; // x is in block scope
    }
    // x is not accessible here
    ```

```

---

### **C**

- **Class**: A user-defined type in C++ that encapsulates data (members) and functions (methods) that operate on that data. Classes are the foundation of object-oriented programming (OOP).

  - Example:

    ```cpp
    class Car {
    private:
        int speed;
    public:
        void setSpeed(int s) {
            speed = s;
        }
        int getSpeed() {

```
        return speed;
    }
};
```

- **Compiler**: A tool that translates C++ source code into machine code (binary executable). Common C++ compilers include GCC, Clang, and MSVC.

- **Constructor**: A special function of a class that is automatically called when an object of the class is created. It initializes the object's members.
  - Example:
  ```cpp
  class MyClass {
  public:
      MyClass() {
          std::cout << "Constructor called!" << std::endl;
      }
  };
```

- **Const**: A keyword that defines constants, or objects whose value cannot be changed after initialization. It can be applied to variables, pointers, function arguments, and class methods.

  - Example:

    ```cpp
    const int maxSize = 100;
    ```

- **Copy Constructor**: A constructor that creates a new object by copying an existing object of the same class. The copy constructor is invoked when passing objects by value or when copying objects.

  - Example:

    ```cpp
    MyClass(const MyClass& other) {
        // Copy constructor
    }
    ```

- **CRTP (Curiously Recurring Template Pattern)**: A design pattern in C++ where a class template is used to inherit from another template, typically allowing for static polymorphism.

  - Example:

    ```cpp
    template <typename Derived>
    class Base {
    public:
        void interface() {
            static_cast<Derived*>(this)->implementation();
        }
    };

    class Derived : public Base<Derived> {
    public:
        void implementation() {
            // Derived-specific code
    ```

        }
    };
    ```

---

### **D**

- **Dangling Pointer**: A pointer that points to a memory location that has been freed or deleted. Dereferencing a dangling pointer leads to undefined behavior.
  - Example:
    ```cpp
    int* ptr = new int(5);
    delete ptr;
    // ptr is now a dangling pointer
    ```

- **Data Member**: Variables declared inside a
    ```

class. These represent the attributes or properties of an object created from that class.

- Example:

```cpp
class Employee {
public:
    int id;
    std::string name;
};
```

- **Destructor**: A special member function of a class that is called when an object is destroyed. It is used to clean up resources (such as memory) that the object may have acquired during its lifetime.

- Example:

```cpp
class MyClass {
public:
    ~MyClass() {
```

```
        std::cout << "Destructor called!" << std::endl;
    }
};
```

- **Dynamic Memory**: Memory that is allocated during program execution (runtime), typically using `new` or `malloc`. Dynamic memory must be manually managed and released using `delete` or `free`.

  - Example:

    ```cpp
    int* ptr = new int[10];  // Allocates an array of 10 integers
    delete[] ptr;            // Releases the memory
    ```

E

- **Encapsulation**: One of the four pillars of object-oriented programming (OOP), encapsulation refers to the bundling of data and methods that operate on the data into a single unit (a class), and restricting access to some of the object's components.

- Example:

```cpp
class Account {
private:
    double balance;
public:
    void deposit(double amount) {
        balance += amount;
    }
    double getBalance() const {
        return balance;
    }
};
```

- **Enumeration (Enum)**: A user-defined type that consists of a set of named integral constants. Enums are used to define variables that can only hold specific values.

  - Example:

    ```cpp
    enum Direction { North, East, South, West };
    Direction dir = North;
    ```

- **Exception Handling**: A mechanism for handling runtime errors in a controlled manner using the `try`, `catch`, and `throw` keywords. It allows you to detect and recover from errors without crashing the program.

  - Example:

    ```cpp
    try {
        throw std::runtime_error("An error occurred");
    } catch (const std::runtime_error& e) {
        std::cout << e.what() << std::endl;
    }
    ```

```

---

### **F**

- **Friend Function**: A function that is not a member of a class but has access to its private and protected members. It is declared using the `friend` keyword inside the class.
  - Example:
  ```cpp
  class MyClass {
  private:
      int data;
  public:
      friend void accessData(MyClass& obj);
  };

  void accessData(MyClass& obj) {
  ```
  ```

    std::cout << obj.data << std::endl;
}
```

- **Function Overloading**: A feature in C++ that allows multiple functions to have the same name, but with different parameter lists (types or number of parameters). The compiler determines which function to call based on the arguments passed.

- Example:

```cpp
int add(int a, int b) {
    return a + b;
}

double add(double a, double b) {
    return a + b;
}
```
```

- **Function Pointer**: A pointer that stores the address of a function. It can be used to call functions indirectly or pass functions as arguments to other functions.

  - Example:

    ```cpp
    int add(int a, int b) {
        return a + b;
    }

    int (*funcPtr)(int, int) = &add;
    int result = funcPtr(5, 3);  // Calls add(5, 3)
    ```

G

-

Garbage Collection: An automatic process of reclaiming memory that is no longer in use. C++ does not have built-in garbage collection, but memory can be managed manually or with **smart pointers**.

- **Generic Programming**: A style of programming where algorithms and data structures are written in a way that they can work with any data type. In C++, **templates** are used to implement generic programming.

  - Example:

    ```cpp
    template <typename T>
    T add(T a, T b) {
        return a + b;
    }
    ```

H

- **Header File**: A file that contains declarations of functions, classes, and variables, typically with a `.h` or `.hpp` extension. Header files allow for modular code and the separation of interface from implementation.

  - Example: `#include <iostream>`

- **Heap**: A region of memory where dynamic memory allocation occurs. In C++, memory allocated with `new` or `malloc` comes from the heap, and must be manually freed.

I

- **Inheritance**: A fundamental concept in object-oriented programming (OOP) where a class (derived class) inherits properties and behaviors (members and methods) from another class (base class). This promotes code reuse.

  - Example:

    ```cpp
    ```

```cpp
class Base {
public:
    void show() {
        std::cout << "Base class" << std::endl;
    }
};

class Derived : public Base {
public:
    void show() {
        std::cout << "Derived class" << std::endl;
    }
};
```

- **Inline Function**: A function that is expanded in place where it is called, rather than being called through the usual function mechanism. This eliminates the overhead of a function call but can increase the size of the binary.

- Example:

  ```cpp
  inline int square(int x) {
      return x * x;
  }
  ```

- **Iterator**: An object that allows traversing a container (like a vector or list) in a sequential manner. Iterators are provided by the **Standard Template Library (STL)**.

  - Example:

  ```cpp
  std::vector<int> v = {1, 2, 3};
  std::vector<int>::iterator it;
  for (it = v.begin(); it != v.end(); ++it) {
      std::cout << *it << " ";
  }
  ```

J

- **Just-In-Time Compilation (JIT)**: A compilation technique where code is compiled during execution rather than before execution. C++ typically uses ahead-of-time compilation rather than JIT.

L

- **Lambda Expression**: An anonymous function that can be defined inline. Lambdas can capture variables from their surrounding scope.
  - Example:

  ```cpp
  auto add = [](int a, int b) {
      return a + b;
  };
  ```

```

- **Lvalue**: An expression that refers to a memory location and allows for assignment. In contrast, an **rvalue** is a temporary value that does not refer to a memory location.

  - Example:

    ```cpp
    int x = 5;  // x is an lvalue
    int y = x;  // x can be assigned to y
    ```

M

- **Macro**: A preprocessor directive that defines a name for a code fragment, often used for constants or small code snippets. Macros are created using `#define`.

  - Example:
    ```

```cpp
#define PI 3.14159
```

- **Move Semantics**: An optimization technique introduced in C++11 that allows resources to be transferred from one object to another without copying. This is done using **rvalue references** and the **move constructor**.

  - Example:

  ```cpp
  class MyClass {
  public:
      MyClass(MyClass&& other) noexcept {
          // Move constructor
      }
  };
  ```

- **Mutex**: A synchronization primitive used to control access to shared resources in multithreaded programs. A mutex ensures that only one thread can access the resource at a time.

- Example:

```cpp
std::mutex mtx;
mtx.lock();
// Critical section
mtx.unlock();
```

N

- **Namespace**: A declarative region that provides a scope to the identifiers (names of types, functions, variables, etc.). Namespaces prevent name collisions in large projects.

- Example:

```cpp
```

```
namespace MyNamespace {

    int myVariable;

}
```

- **Null Pointer**: A pointer that does not point to any object or valid memory location. In C++, a null pointer can be represented using `nullptr`.

  - Example:

  ```cpp
  int* ptr = nullptr;
  ```

O

- **Object**: An instance of a class. In C++, objects represent entities that contain data (attributes) and behaviors (methods).

- Example:

```cpp
Car myCar; // myCar is an object of class Car
```


- **Operator Overloading**: A feature that allows developers to define custom behavior for operators when they are applied to objects of a class. This improves the readability and usability of user-defined types.

- Example:

```cpp
class Complex {
public:
    Complex operator+(const Complex& other) {
        // Define behavior for + operator
    }
};
```

P

- **Pointer**: A variable that stores the memory address of another variable. Pointers allow for dynamic memory management and low-level memory manipulation.

  - Example:

    ```cpp
    int x = 5;
    int* ptr = &x; // ptr points to the address of x
    ```

- **Polymorphism**: The ability to use a single interface to represent different types or classes. In C++, polymorphism is typically achieved through **virtual functions** and inheritance.

  - Example:

    ```cpp
    class Base {
    ```

```cpp
public:
    virtual void show() {
        std::cout << "Base class" << std::endl;
    }
};

class Derived : public Base {
public:
    void show() override {
        std::cout << "Derived class" << std::endl;
    }
};
```

Q

- **Queue**: A container that follows the **First In

First Out (FIFO)** principle. C++ provides `std::queue` in the **STL**.

- Example:

```cpp
std::queue<int> q;
q.push(1);
q.push(2);
q.pop(); // Removes 1
```

R

- **RAII (Resource Acquisition Is Initialization)**: A programming idiom in C++ where resources (such as memory, file handles, etc.) are acquired and released using objects' constructors and destructors.

- Example:

```cpp
```

```cpp
class FileHandler {
public:
    FileHandler(const std::string& fileName) {
        file = std::fopen(fileName.c_str(), "r");
    }
    ~FileHandler() {
        if (file) std::fclose(file);
    }
private:
    FILE* file;
};
```

- **Rvalue**: An expression that represents a temporary value that cannot be assigned to. Rvalues typically refer to expressions that are used in operations but do not have a persistent memory location.

S

- **Smart Pointer**: A C++ object that wraps around a raw pointer to manage the pointer's lifetime automatically. Smart pointers such as `std::unique_ptr`, `std::shared_ptr`, and `std::weak_ptr` are used to prevent memory leaks and dangling pointers.

  - Example:

    ```cpp
    std::unique_ptr<int> ptr = std::make_unique<int>(5);
    ```

- **Static Member**: A class member (either a variable or a function) that is shared among all instances of the class. Static members belong to the class itself rather than to any individual object.

  - Example:

    ```cpp
    class MyClass {
    ```

```cpp
public:
    static int count;
};
```

- **Stack**: A region of memory used for static memory allocation, typically for function calls and local variables. The **stack** is managed automatically and follows a **Last In First Out (LIFO)** structure.

T

- **Template**: A feature that allows functions and classes to operate with generic types, enabling code reuse for different data types. Templates are the foundation of **generic programming** in C++.
  - Example:
  ```cpp
  template <typename T>
  ```

```cpp
T add(T a, T b) {
    return a + b;
}
```

- **Thread**: A unit of execution within a program. C++11 introduced threading support via the `<thread>` library, enabling parallel execution of code.

- Example:

```cpp
std::thread t([](){
    std::cout << "Thread running" << std::endl;
});
t.join();  // Waits for the thread to finish
```

U

- **Unary Operator**: An operator that operates on a single operand. Common unary operators include `++` (increment), `--` (decrement), and `-` (negation).

  - Example:

    ```cpp
    int x = 5;
    x++; // Unary increment operator
    ```

- **Unique Pointer**: A type of **smart pointer** that owns and manages a resource exclusively. `std::unique_ptr` ensures that only one pointer points to a resource at any given time, preventing multiple ownership.

  - Example:

    ```cpp
    std::unique_ptr<int> ptr = std::make_unique<int>(5);
    ```

V

- **Virtual Function**: A function in a base class that can be overridden by derived classes. When a function is declared `virtual`, the C++ runtime determines which function to call based on the object type, enabling **polymorphism**.

  - Example:

    ```cpp
    class Base {
    public:
        virtual void show() {
            std::cout << "Base class" << std::endl;
        }
    };
    ```

- **Vector**: A dynamic array provided by the **STL** that can resize automatically as elements are added or removed. `std::vector` is commonly used for storing collections of elements.

  - Example:

    ```cpp
    std::vector<int> v = {1, 2, 3};
    v.push_back(4); // Adds 4 to the vector
    ```

W

- **Weak Pointer**: A type of **smart pointer** that does not participate in the ownership of an object, allowing objects to be referenced without preventing them from being destroyed. `std::weak_ptr` is used to avoid **circular references** in shared ownership scenarios.

  - Example:

    ```cpp
    std::weak_ptr<int> weakPtr = sharedPtr;
    ```

Z

- **Zero Initialization**: The process of initializing variables to zero. For example, a global or static variable with no initializer is zero-initialized by default in C++.

This glossary provides foundational terms and concepts in C++, designed to be a reference guide for both beginners and experienced programmers. The terminology plays a critical role in understanding the language, its features, and how to use it effectively in various programming paradigms.

Index

1. Introduction pg.4

2. Basics of C++ Programming pg.26

3. Functions in C++ pg.47

4. Object-Oriented Programming in C++ pg.70

5. Advanced C++ Features pg.96

6. The Standard Template Library pg.123

7. File Input/Output in C++ pg.146

8. Multithreading and Concurrency in C++ pg.168

9.Best Practices and Design Patterns in C++ pg.192

10.C++ Glossary pg.219

www.ingramcontent.com/pod-product-compliance
Lightning Source LLC
Chambersburg PA
CBHW052144220526
45471CB00004B/1522